What people are saying about …

more

"Yes! My heart leaped as I read *More* because it marries the head with the heart. Simon Ponsonby skillfully explains how Christians can have the Holy Spirit … and still need more. Then he leads the reader to the river where they can drink from the waters of renewal for themselves. This book whets my thirst for more of the Holy Spirit."

Michael J. Klassen, author of
Strange Fire, Holy Fire

"Simon Ponsonby is one of the best student chaplains Oxford has ever had. Highly intelligent and winsome, he is a compelling preacher. His first book courageously tackles the foolish divide between 'charismatic' and 'non-charismatic' Christians, urging us all to go deeper with God and expect more from His hand, a more that is not just a one-off experience but an ongoing infusion of God's life, based on the promises of Scripture. This book is full of superb quotations from Christians down the ages and is illuminated by many personal stories. This is required reading, particularly in the conservative and charismatic evangelical camps."

Michael Green, senior research fellow,
Wycliffe Hall, Oxford University

"Simon's book, written out of weakness and born out of longing, will lead the reader, if he humbly asks, straight into more of that encounter with God that changes lives, families, cities, and nations. We live in a day when churches and Christians of all kinds are clogged with materialism and glutted with information but starved and thirsting for an encounter with God. May this book provoke the whole spectrum of the body of Christ to hunger for and experience more of Him."

Charlie Cleverly, author of *The Discipline of Intimacy*

"There are many who emphasize the Word but neglect the Spirit. There are also many who emphasize the Spirit but neglect the Word. There are few who keep both in balance, but Simon Ponsonby is one of the few. With the help of this book, the few may hopefully become the many."

Mark Stibbe, author of *One Touch from the King Changes Everything* and *Prophetic Evangelism*

"This is a most welcome book. Very readable, very responsible, and very well researched. It will certainly whet the appetite for 'something more.'"

David Pytches, bishop of the Anglican Communion and author of *Come Holy Spirit*

"Ponsonby invites us to swim 'in the deep end' of God's love. With a preacher's art and a pastor's heart, he gives us a readable, moving, and direct book. You will finish it with a fresh sense that, with God, there is always more to discover, more to enjoy, more to come."

Jeremy Begbie, Thomas A. Langford research professor, Duke Divinity School, Duke University

"Simon is a passionate man with a big brain and an even bigger heart. Even if you don't agree with everything in this book, I'm sure you'll be moved by it to look deeper into the Bible to test your understanding of God's truth and deeper into your heart to examine the depth of your knowledge of God's love and power."

Vaughan Roberts, rector of St. Ebbe's Church, Oxford

+

simon ponsonby

< more

how you can have more of the Spirit when you already have everything in Christ

David C Cook®

transforming lives together

MORE
Published by David C Cook
4050 Lee Vance View
Colorado Springs, CO 80918 U.S.A.

David C Cook Distribution Canada
55 Woodslee Avenue, Paris, Ontario, Canada N3L 3E5

David C Cook U.K., Kingsway Communications
Eastbourne, East Sussex BN23 6NT, England

The graphic circle C logo is a registered trademark of David C Cook.

The Web site addresses recommended throughout this book are offered as a
resource to you. These Web sites are not intended in any way to be or imply an
endorsement on the part of David C Cook, nor do we vouch for their content.

Unless otherwise indicated, all Scripture quotations are the author's own
translation. Scripture quotations marked NASB are taken from the *New American
Standard Bible*, © Copyright 1960, 1995 by The Lockman Foundation. Used
by permission. Scripture quotations marked ESV are taken from *The Holy
Bible, English Standard Version*. Copyright © 2000; 2001 by Crossway Bibles,
a division of Good News Publishers. Used by permission. All rights reserved.
Scripture quotations marked NIV are taken from the *Holy Bible, New International
Version*®. NIV®. Copyright © 1973, 1978, 1984 International Bible Society. Used
by permission of Zondervan. All rights reserved. Scripture quotations marked
KJV taken from the King James Version of the Bible. (Public Domain.)

LCCN 2009927177
ISBN 978-1-4347-6538-3
eISBN 978-1-4347-0036-0

The Team: Melanie Larson, Amy Kiechlin, Sarah Schultz, and Jaci Schneider
Study Questions: Karen Lee-Thorp
Cover Design: David Carlson, Studio Gearbox
Cover Photo: Getty Images, Roy Hsu, UpperCut Images Collection, rights-managed

Printed in the United States of America
Second Edition 2009

2 3 4 5 6 7 8 9 10 11

081514-LS

Dedicated to those who minister "more" in word and Spirit:

Pastor Jeffrey Ponsonby

Canon John Simons

Reverend Sue Rose

Canon David MacInnes

CONTENTS

INTRODUCTION

A FISH IN TROUBLE

"So this is a River!"

"THE River," corrected the Rat.

"And you really live by the river? What a jolly life."

"By it, and with it, and on it, and in it," said the Rat.

*"It's brother and sister to me, and aunts and
company and food and drink and (naturally)
washing. It's my world, and I don't want any other.
What it hasn't got is not worth having and what it
doesn't know is not worth knowing! Lord! The times
we've had together."*[1]

The day began with my quiet time, when I sensed the Lord telling me that today would be a special day in which He was going to speak importantly to me. I wrote this in my journal and went into the day expectant. I was on holiday in Normandy with my wife, Tiffany, and our two boys, Nathanael and Joel, and we had a wonderful day. We spent it at the majestic Mont-Saint-Michel and were deeply moved by participating in the sublime eucharistic worship in the abbey. I felt close to the Lord and was moved to tears by His presence.

Several hours later, back at our holiday cottage, I lay on the bed reflecting on the day at Mont-Saint-Michel and on what the Lord might be saying, while Tiffany and the boys went to feed the fish in the pond at the bottom of the garden. This was no ordinary-sized pond and these were no ordinary sized goldfish! Some of the carp had grown to a massive eighteen inches and weighed ten pounds.

Suddenly Tiffany's voice called out anxiously, "Simon, come quick, there's a fish in trouble!" Somewhat bemused, I rushed to the end of the garden, and there, stuck in the sand in a few inches of water, was a massive orange, black, and silver carp with a girth like a sumo wrestler. Perhaps it had followed some tasty morsel into the shallows, or perhaps this was its favorite spot. Unfortunately this fish had not reckoned on the abnormally hot weather and low rainfall. The water in the pond was twice as shallow as usual—and this noble fish was out of its depth. In trying to wriggle back towards deeper and safer water, the fish had only become further embedded in the sand, gills partly above water, slowly suffocating to death.

I climbed into the pond, perched on an exposed stone, and attempted to nudge the fish with a stick towards deeper water. This probably only annoyed my fish even more, and ultimately proved futile. I feared damaging it by picking it up and manhandling it across the pond. Somewhat inspired, I asked Tiffany to get a trashcan lid and a watering can. Pouring water on the fish offered momentary

relief, then I levered that huge fish onto the trashcan lid and, straining, I carried it to the deeper end where I plonked it back into the
water. Tiffany and the boys held their own breaths, as the fish lay
there in the water, momentarily motionless and fighting to breathe.
Then suddenly it seemed to lunge to life: With a swipe of its tail
and a cocky splash, it found its bearings and, in a flash of orange,
black, and silver, turned and swam for the deep end. I puffed out my
chest and swaggered like an Olympic gold-medal sprinter, milking
the applause from my impressed family.

Almost immediately, as we headed back to the cottage, I sensed
the Lord speaking to me. *The church is like that carp: mature, distinguished, and impressive. She has lived long, fought hard, eaten well. But
she has left or been lured out of the deep waters. And here she is stuck
in the mud and suffocating. Occasional momentary relief from the odd
spiritual watering cannot save her. Her only hope is to get back to deep
water.* This was what the Lord had promised to give me—a revelation
of His heart's concern for His church in distress, out of her depth.[2]

That evening, my multicolored carp was seen playing around in
the deep end. Its fellow fish, however, had not learned from the near
disaster. I was hugely disappointed when I returned on successive
days to see other giant, noble fish, having made the same mistake,
without anyone there to help, lying dead in the shallows.

Many Christians have tragically departed from the deep waters
of God's life-giving Spirit and, like fish out of water, they are slowly
suffocating. Whatever the circumstances that have led to them end-
ing up in the shallows, stuck in the sand, gasping for life—whether
it be false theology, poor discipleship, willful sin, or simply the exigencies of life in a broken world—God is willing and working for

His church to be moved back into the deep waters of His life. What is required is not a stick (perhaps representing judgment, rebuke, punishment, or chastisement) to prod these troubled fish along, nor the odd sprinkling of water from a can (perhaps representing the occasional spiritual fix of a renewal meeting, conference, or ministry session) to give superficial relief to a critical predicament, but a sustained, permanent immersion in the deep end. Relocation to the deep end may be unexpected, awkward, and outside our previous experience (that carp had never been in a trashcan lid before), but desperate times call for desperate measures. And the church is in desperate times. Yet God is at work, teaching us about the deep, and exhorting us to have a biblical expectation of life in the deep. He is drawing His fish back to where they can breathe and thrive, where they belong, in the deep waters of the life of His Spirit.

This book is for those of us who are fed up with flapping around in the shallows. It is for those who long to swim in the deep waters of the life of God. It seeks to offer both a biblical direction for and a biblical description of the deep end. I hope also that it echoes something of God's invitation, His longing heart beckoning us to Him.

> *Rush from the demons*
> *for my King has found me,*
> *Leap from the universe*
> *And plunge in Thee.*[3]

CHAPTER 1

LONGING FOR THE DEEP

Many Christians are unaware that a deep end exists. They have become so used to living in the shallows that they think this is the norm. Perhaps this is not all they expected when they were first born into the pond, but they are generally content to paddle until they get to the big pond in the sky. Occasionally they hear rumors that there is a deep end, they meet the odd person who claims to have come from the deep end, one or two of their fellow shallow-enders have even left them and said they are off to the deep, and every now and again they wonder, *So how do I get to this deep end?* Or perhaps you're like that beautiful carp: gasping and desperate for the deeper waters. Like the pope in Robert Browning's poem "The Ring and the Book," you're crying, "Well, is the thing we see, salvation?"

Billy Graham once wrote,

> *Everywhere I go I find that God's people lack something. They are hungry for something. Their Christian experience is not all that they expected and they often have recurring defeat in their lives. Christians today are hungry for spiritual fulfillment. The*

most desperate need of the nation today is that men and women
who profess Jesus be filled with the Holy Spirit.[1]

Billy Graham's global itinerant ministry perhaps gave him a better
insight into the condition of the church than any other twentieth-
century Christian leader. First, he rightly identifies the desperation
in the lives of many Christians. Second, he suggests that a failing
church has implications for influencing the nation. Third, he offers a
resolution—immersion in the Holy Spirit.

It is because of these first two insights, desperation in our lives
and a failing church, that I have written this book about the resolution, the water for our gasping lungs: God's Holy Spirit. It is my
intention throughout this book to deduce from Scripture and the
church's testimony the reality of an essential, personal, tangible,
repeatable Pentecost. We are searching for that place of encounter,
depth, and intimacy with God—that place of power to serve, that
place of character to conform us to Christ, that place from which
we may live, move, and have our being in the fullness of the Holy
Spirit.

THERE MUST BE MORE!

Johann Christoph Blumhardt was responsible for steering an extraordinary awakening in his little village of Mottlingen, Germany, in the
late nineteenth century. Accompanied by signs and wonders, this
renewal sent shock waves throughout the country, and many thousands traveled to the village specifically to meet God, confess their
sins, and find personal spiritual renewal. As with Billy Graham in the

following century, Blumhardt incisively recognized that the church was asleep, wretched, lukewarm, blind, and poor, living below her birthright, failing herself and her Master and the lost world, because she had failed to avail herself of all that the Holy Spirit would, could, and should bring. The key to Blumhardt's authority and influence stemmed from his discontent with the status quo of spirituality, and from his persistent prayer for and pursuit of the depth of the Holy Spirit. Listen to him on his knees, beseeching God for more:

> *I long for another outpouring of the Holy Spirit, another Pentecost. That must come if things are to change in Christianity, for it simply cannot continue in such a wretched state. The gifts and powers of the early Christian time—Oh how I long for their return. And I believe the savior is just waiting for us to ask for them … When I look at what we have, I cannot help sighing … Oh Lord Jesus is that the promised Spirit for which you hung on a tree? Where is the Spirit that penetrates nation after nation as swiftly as at the time of the apostles and places them at Jesus' feet?*[2]

This prayer, this pursuit, this rediscovered power, brought deliverance to the captives, salvation to the lost, and renewed hope and joy to the believers. It also shook the nation, prophetically challenging the inexorable advance of a bloodless, Bible-less, God-less liberal Protestant theology.

One of the great expositors of the church, Dr. Martyn Lloyd-Jones, once thundered at those Christians who claim to have it all, who claim that there is nothing more of God to receive and experience, "Got it all? I simply ask in the name of God, why then are you as you are? If you have got it all, why are you so unlike the New Testament Christians? Got it all? Got it all at your conversion? Well where is it, I ask?"[3] His point is incisive: If we have what the first Christians had, why do we not do what they did? We must conclude that either God gave them more than He has given us, or we have failed to avail ourselves of what He has given us.

Lloyd-Jones was thinking particularly of what he and others call "baptism in the Spirit," a term that I hesitate to use.[4] He believed that this was a specific experience, often following conversion, which was repeatable, definite, tangible, and manifested in some particular, sensorily perceptible manner. It issues in changed countenance, bold speech, and specific gifting. It produces deep assurance—beyond mere assent to truth at conversion—that we are children of God and ultimately directs attention away from the recipient to Christ.[5] The strident Calvinist John Piper, in a sermon series on Acts,[6] has similarly spoken of baptism in the Spirit as "an overwhelming experience of the greatness of God, spilling over in courageous passionate praise and worship."

My main hesitation with this teaching, although I do not question the reality of the experience, is that it is too often reduced to a once-only experience, subsequent to conversion—although Lloyd-Jones believed it was repeatable. I believe this encounter may be initially consciously "experienced" with conversion (see Acts 19:6f.; 10:44f.) or subsequent to conversion (see Acts 2; 8:4f.; 9:17). It may be an overwhelming event or a progressively deepening encounter. At the swimming pool, my son Nathanael jumps into the deep end, while I prefer to lower myself in more slowly. The net result is the

same, however; we know we are in the water and not on the edge.
I simply do not believe it is a once-only "second blessing" (another
term I will not use). It is, rather, a constantly repeatable, deepening
experience of God's Spirit, who brings a greater revelation of the
person and work of Christ, a blazing love for Christ, a greater and
more effective empowering witness to Christ, and a transforming
conformity to the character of Christ.

For instance, I remember well the first time I kissed my wife,
Tiffany, on the eve of our engagement, but it was not to be the
last time! If it had been the only time, I would have been the most
delighted of men, and it would have been memorable—but, praise
God, it was not unique, just the memorable start of even greater
things and a deeper intimacy to come. So I believe in the baptisms of
the Spirit, the fillings with the Spirit, the anointings of the Spirit, the
ever-increasing, ever-deepening immersion into God. Bishop David
Pytches famously said, "Yes, I believe in the second blessing—it
comes after the first and before the third."

If one wants specifically to name such an experience and such a
life, which I believe is the recognition and activation of the Spirit who
dwells within every believer (Eph. 1:13; 4:13), then I think something
like "filled with the fullness" would be more biblically legitimate. Paul
reveals this dynamic tension of being filled with what we are full of
in Colossians 2:10, where he says that through Christ we are filled
with the fullness of Christ. However, in Colossians 1:9f., he prays that
they may be filled with the Spirit of wisdom and revelation, that they
might know and serve Him better, bearing fruit and being empowered by the might of His glory. In Ephesians 1:23, Paul says that we,
His body the church, are filled with the fullness of Christ, but he also

prays in Ephesians 3:19 that we may be filled with the fullness of God and exhorts us in 5:18 to be filled with the Spirit.

This ongoing experience of God is the longing of so many Christians, the need of the nations, and the gift of God through Christ by His Spirit. But unless we are, like the psalmist (Ps. 42:1f.), consumed by desire for the streams of the living God, the chances are we will never know how these waters satiate and we will live our Christian life parched and cracked and trying in the flesh to hang in there until we reach heaven. Unless we are filled by the living waters of the Holy Spirit, which Jesus promised would flow out, not in (John 7:38), we will never be the blessing God intended us to be. We will never water and transform the dead and barren deserts around us into life, as we see with the river that flowed from the temple, turning the salty seawater fresh (Ezek. 47:8).

A POWERFUL TRADITION OF "MORE"

Recently I have been gripped by a worship song by Tim Hughes called "Consuming Fire," which has captured the hearts of many in articulating their yearning for more of God. Beginning with the line, "There must be more than this: O Breath of God, come breathe within," this prayer in song invokes the Holy Spirit to come and establish in us a greater sense of God's presence, a greater anointing of power, a greater deliverance from bondage, and a greater release in worship. This theme should always be a prayerful song on the church's heart and lips. Tim Hughes' contemporary song has a long pedigree. One of the most ancient and beloved hymns, "Veni Creator Spiritus," comes from the ninth century and was written by Archbishop Maurus, a devout monk and noted theologian who knew the need in the church for an ongoing Pentecost:

> *Come, Creator Spirit,*
> *Visit the minds of those who are yours.*
> *Fill with heavenly grace*
> *The hearts that you have made.*[7]

This prayer in song continues by asking for a visitation and extension of the work of the Spirit, inflaming our devotion, transforming our characters, equipping our service with gifts and power, enlightening our minds, filling our hearts with love, delivering us from darkness, directing our paths, and entering us into intimate union with God. The authority of the hymn is seen by its unique usage across a millennium and as the only Roman hymn adopted by all Protestant denominations. But for far too long the church has been singing such songs without intention, expectation, or appropriation. We must learn to sing these songs, not out of tradition, but in travail, longing for and begging God to visit us.

Many church luminaries knew they did not have it all and longed for a closer, fuller walk with their Lord. Marked by holy discontent, their search was not in vain. Their experience of more of God was made evident in personal delight, strengthening to the church, salvation to the lost, and glory to God. We can point to John Wesley who, after years of fruitless gospel ministry and personal moral defeat, had his heart "strangely warmed" by God's anointing at Aldersgate in May 1738.[8] Immediately he sensed he had moved from the faith of a slave to the faith of a son, and with this newfound anointing he subsequently shook the nations with apostolic authority. In 1721, Jonathan Edwards entered a season of experiences of God, beholding the loveliness and beauty of Christ. Given a deep revelation of the majesty and meekness of Christ, he was "swallowed up in God." These experiences set the trajectory for his whole life and issued in the precipitation of the New England Awakening and his massive production of some of the most significant and respected theological works in the church. D. L. Moody, already an established and effective minister in Chicago, recalled the street in New York where, in 1871, following a time of deep crying out for more of God's Spirit, he had such an encounter with God that he was never the same again: "One day—oh what a day—God revealed himself to me." His subsequent evangelistic ministry in America and the United Kingdom, particularly London and Cambridge, was marked by many significant conversions. The most effective evangelist in the twentieth-century church, Billy Graham, drew the attention of the woman who would become his wife when both were students at Wheaton College. She said, "There was a seriousness about him; there was a depth ... he was a man who knew God; he was a man who had a purpose, a dedication in his life; he knew where he was going. He wanted to please God more than any man I'd ever known."[9] Such consecration, devotion, and passion for God brought a rent heaven over this man's life and ministry. One man's pursuit of God can influence the nations for God. For all these men this would not be the end of their search for more of God, but they would never settle for less.

One could argue that in each case this was a special anointing, for a special person, at a special time. Perhaps—but it could equally be argued that it was the anointing which made these ordinary men extraordinary. That said, what these notable persons experienced was what hundreds of anonymous folk also equally experienced along with the famous apostles at Pentecost (Acts 2). It was what all the unnamed experienced when the Spirit came to Cornelius's household (Acts 10). It was the same for the nameless converts at Samaria (Acts 8) and for the nameless converts at Ephesus (Acts 19). Thus, while the experience may make some exceptional in God's purposes, the actual experience is not exceptional.

Additionally, while these particular experiences by these particular men were of particular remembrance, a study of the lives of such men shows that experiences like these were not always unique for them and that these men continued to encounter similar experiences. And it is this that we are after: the ongoing experience, the ever-deepening intimacy with our Father.

NO MORE—ENOUGH IS ENOUGH

Some years ago I gave a series of talks on Ephesians at a conference. I noticed after one talk that I was not being received well by certain individuals who were telling others I was not "sound." During my talk on Ephesians 1:15f., which I had called "More," one person in the front row actually groaned and was so manifestly irritated and indignant that I had to ask him to calm down and wait until I had finished. When I met with him afterward, he expressed concern that I was teaching false doctrine. I was flabbergasted. Brought up as a strict Baptist with Plymouth Brethren influence, I regarded myself as a conservative evangelical touched by renewal. I was giving a detailed exegesis of Ephesians based on the Greek text—but clearly I had said something deemed to be heresy. It turns out that the whole issue had been brought about by my assertion that Paul had a double perspective in Ephesians: What they have in Christ and what they may have in Christ. Clearly my challenger did not believe there was anything more to be had.

Those who question whether there is anything "more" do so for several reasons:

1. They think that to speak of "more" undermines the finished work of Calvary.

2. They think that the presentation of "more" means only "second blessing," and view this as unscriptural, elitist, and Gnostic.

3. They think that to teach or expect "more" is to inculcate the egocentric, materialistic, hedonistic, consumerist mentality of the late twentieth and early twenty-first centuries.

4. They think such teaching is an abstraction from the Great Commission, in which we end up focused on spiritual frisson rather than on sending mission.

5. They think that, like the Corinthians, we are guilty of overrealized eschatology and need to be brought back to basics.

6. They think that, like the Colossians, such teaching is an addition to the gospel and is therefore a subtraction from the gospel.

7. They think that to speak of "more" is a sign of immaturity, even insecurity, in one's faith, and a failing to appreciate the finished work of the cross. Indeed, some suggest that those who ask for more ask because they may not have Christ already.

Now, these are all important points, not without some basis, which charismatics must respond to and make sure they are not prone to. Throughout this book I will try to address them. While we must heed these concerns, however, those who protest the notion of "more" must heed our questions too.

Is it possible that those who reject the charismatic experience do so because of one or more of the points outlined below?

1. Perhaps they are selective in their reading of Scripture—biblically reductionist. They read Scripture through a narrow theological filter and, while making the cross central, actually fail to see that the cross is the door, not the room.

2. Perhaps they themselves are deficient in their experience of the Spirit and make their inadequate experience the sole basis for what is sound.

3. Perhaps their own emotional, sociological, psychological, and theological matrix has made them suspicious of experience, feelings, and emotions.

4. Perhaps they have absorbed the rationalist Enlightenment mind-set, and they want to put God in a theological, hermeneutical, dogmatic box, not realizing that the Spirit blows where He wills and breaks out of boxes.

5. Perhaps they function from what I term a "biblical deism"—God being absent from the world apart from His word written, read, or heralded.

6. Perhaps they are truly satisfied with their religion—but is this reduced to gratitude for salvation, giving the gospel, and gritting their teeth till glory?

7. Perhaps, like several who have confided in me, they have

asked for the gifts of the Spirit, often particularly tongues, and when their request appeared unanswered, hope deferred made the heart sick. So, out of pain and a sense of rejection, they became angry, resentful, and ultimately dismissive of things charismatic.

My own understanding follows that expressed by the evangelical preacher and writer Vaughan Roberts, who recently told me, "In Christ we have everything, but manifestly we aren't living in light of all we've received in Christ." Amen. What I am calling for, what I believe God is inviting us into, is simply what has been achieved for us by Christ at the cross. More, not something over and above the cross, not an optional extra or a reward for good behavior, but the ongoing reception of the benefits of the cross. We need to work out God's working in us (Phil. 2:12b–13). We may taste now of the powers of the age to come (Heb. 6:4)—we may enter partially into God's kingdom come.

Emil Brunner rightly noted, "At every period in the history of the Church the greatest sin of the Church, and the one which caused the greatest distress, is that she withholds the Gospel from the world and, herself."[10] I am not advocating graduating from the gospel to some pseudo-Gnostic higher life. Quite the contrary. I am advocating appropriating the gospel. But this gospel is more than the "Four Spiritual Laws" or "Two Ways to Live."[11] It is more than a turning aside of God's righteous wrath deserved by us and a substitution of Christ in our place (Rom. 3:23f.), more than a guarantee of sins forgiven and entry into heaven when we die. It is all that, but it is more than that: It is the implication of that, the outworking of that.

That is the start, not the finish. That is the way opened up to return to Eden (Rev. 22:1f.), the red carpet in Christ's blood that leads us home to the Father's embrace and kiss for the prodigal (Luke 15:20). It is the shedding abroad of God's love in our hearts (Rom. 5); it is a baptism into the triune life of God, that we might be in Him as Christ lives in us (John 17:21); it is the adoring recognition from the depths of our being that God is "Abba," our dear Father (Rom. 8:15f.). It is liberation from bondage, and transformation from one degree of glory into the likeness of Christ, and this by the Spirit (2 Cor. 3).

One Christmas morning, my reading was Matthew 7:11—"If you being evil know how to give good gifts to your children, how much more will your heavenly Father give good gifts to those who ask." It seemed a perfect Christmas text. That day my family went to church where we celebrated the greatest gift of God. Then, as is customary in the Ponsonby household, we ate our Christmas dinner and listened to the queen's annual speech before opening our Christmas presents. I had bought both my sons giant LEGO and BRIO castles. They grabbed these huge parcels, ripped open the wrapping, and immediately began exploring the pieces and the instruction manuals to assemble their castles. After several minutes my mother-in-law piped up, "There are still more presents under the tree!" She was right. There were in fact numerous other presents under the tree that all went with the castles—dragons and knights and battering rams and treasure chests and scaling ladders, etc. They weren't the main gift—the castles were—but they were carefully chosen, bought and paid for, lovingly wrapped and labeled, to be enjoyed along with the castles. It didn't take long for my boys to grab what was theirs and start enjoying it. The main gift of God is salvation through the Christ event. But under that barbarous beautiful tree of Calvary are many other wonderful rights and promises and privileges and gifts that go with God's main gift to us.

This desire for more of God is a sign of spiritual health. The mature want more. We recognize that a marriage where one partner no longer desires more intimacy is in trouble, that a baby who no longer wants to eat is sick, that a bird that no longer wants to fly is crippled—and so we must recognize also that a Christian who no longer wants to know, grow, hear, see, touch, serve, love, and be changed by God is also in trouble, sick, and crippled. "The more I have, the more I want" is not merely a reflection of twenty-first-century consumerism, but rather the authentic cry of the true believer. I believe that the desire for more of God is not only part of the essential DNA of the spiritual life, but also mirrors the natural desire of the heart of God. As a father longs to spend time with his children, or a lover longs to spend time with his bride, so the loving Father God is longing for us, pursuing us, not content with all that He has of us.

All the great Western thinkers, from Augustine through Anselm and Richard of St. Victor to the medieval mystics, spoke of the Holy Spirit as personified love between Father and Son, sent as a gift to unite us in love to God, to one another, and in love to embrace the world with the gospel.[12] Christianity was never meant to be merely a meal ticket to heaven and a disciplined gritting of the teeth until the day we get there. Rather now, today, by the Spirit, we are seated with Him in heavenly realms (Eph. 2:6), the beloved leaning on His breast (John 13:23).

IN MY EXPERIENCE

I purposely emphasize the word "experience" and will seek to show from Scripture the importance of experience. A nonexperiential religion is suspect, for it fails to deal with the totality of our being. Eduard Schweizer said, "Long before the Holy Spirit became an article of the creed, [He] was a living reality in the experience of the primitive church."[13] Authentic Christianity will engage with and evoke a response from our heart, soul, strength, and mind (Deut. 6:5; Matt. 22:37). That is every aspect of our being: emotional, spiritual, physical, and intellectual. We must challenge any attempts to exorcise experience from Christianity, reducing it to something fiduciary. When this occurs, we become the flip side of liberalism—post-Enlightenment rationalists who define our foundations as merely intellectual beings, minds: "I think therefore I am." I believe there is a danger that some evangelicals may operate on just such a rationalist hermeneutic,[14] only they would say that the miraculous and the marvelous experiences of God were for the biblical time only. In this they have failed to see how the doctrinal impacts the existential. Mark Stibbe remarked to me that if the dentist tells us, as he sets about drilling, "You won't feel this," we should question the truthfulness of his statement; similarly, when some Christians say, "You won't feel this," we should quickly challenge that statement.

I am not suggesting that sought or claimed experience of God is self-validating, although the twelfth-century mystic monk Bernard of Clairvaux rightly added to Anselm's "Credo ut intelligam" ("I believe in order that I may know") the balance, "Credo ut experiar" ("I believe that I may experience"). Commenting on the Song of Solomon, for him an allegory of the Christian union with Christ,

Bernard declared that only the experience of the Spirit could teach one to sing this sort of song.[15] Bernard was clear that many Christian monks had not experienced the invasion of God's love and grace. For Bernard, experience was a form of evidence, but it was also clear to him, as it should be for us, that such experiences, although authoritative, might sometimes be deceptive or at least misunderstood, and were to be subjected to the norms of Scripture and faith.

William of St. Thierry, a young Cistercian mystic who wrote passionately on the nature of Christian experience of the love of God by the Spirit of God, spoke of "knowing by experience," which was not a question of mere logic taught in school, but of encounter. The control for Thierry was that the experience flowed from a salvation economy trajectory, as follows: The Trinity (one God in three persons)—Christology (Christ at the center)—pneumatology (Spirit at the center)—love (for humankind)—knowledge (via Scripture/church)—experience. It was thus not a detached experience, but one that tied the individual into the life of God.[16] It was a rich, deep, personal, and wonderful experience of being loved. Experience in a felt communion with God was crucial to Puritan spirituality. They spoke of "experimental" theology, meaning what we would term today "experiential." Puritan scholar Geoffrey Nuttall said theirs was "a movement to immediacy in relation to God."

The very safeguard of Scripture speaks of experience as the norm of the religious life. We are born again by the Spirit of God—transformed into new creatures, adopted as sons of God. What is that if it is not an experience? The Spirit pours out the love of God in our hearts. What is that if it is not an experience? The believers were filled with the Spirit and preached spontaneously. What is that if it is not an experience? Those evangelicals who are wary of an experiential Christianity must demonstrate from Scripture that our relationship with God is an existentially, emotionally detached, intellectual act of faith. In fact it is not a question of either/or, but of both/and. I love the title of Henry Rack's biography of John Wesley, *Reasonable Enthusiast*, implying as it does the union of reason and deep emotional experience.

Jonathan Edwards, perhaps the foremost American academic of his era and the greatest preacher and revivalist, wrote a full treatise on the importance of "affections" in religion.[17] He begins his discussion with the text from 1 Peter 1:8 speaking of our "rejoicing with unspeakable joy and full of glory." Whatever else these affections are, they are so profound a feeling such as cannot be articulated with the mind and mouth.

Our experience by the Spirit is an experience of God the Spirit. Therefore we should expect that the Spirit's divine attributes and predicates somehow define our experience of Him. He cannot mediate something other than His being—love, power, holiness, self-giving, Christ-centering. Even metaphors that describe Him may give an indication of how we experience Him: gentle dove, purging fire, elusive wind, cleansing satiating water, strengthening comforter. We may expect "mountaintop" experiences of God, but we must also expect to experience God in the mundane. Encounters may be a divine transcendence, but they may also include a sense of divine absence. Most common will be a subtle accompanying presence through the long, hard, faithful road of obedience. But I believe that an inner witness, a felt Christ, a known belief, is to be normative. Brian Gaybba says, "Mountain-top experiences pass away. But love and the fruits of love remain as the way in which the Spirit is experienced."[18] Romans 5:5 and 1 Corinthians 13 show this to be true—Christ's love experienced, His love expressed.

Finally, in all our desire for more experience of God, we must be careful that we do not fall victim to a subjectivism divorced from objective, rational, biblical truth. Our relationship with God can seldom deepen without the Bible, but that relationship is with God and not with the Bible. As we will see, encounter with God is both through propositional revelation accessed by reading Scripture and hearing sermons, and through existential revelation. There is both intellectual acknowledgment and emotional, spiritual engagement. It is not either/or, but both/and. The two do not compete with each other; they complement each other. Is this not what the apostle Paul meant when he said, "I know whom I have believed" (2 Tim. 1:12 NIV)? He did not mean "know about," but "truly know." The question for us is, can we say the same? The more we receive of the Spirit, the more we will know the Savior.

A BATH-FULL OR A BASIN?

Some may ask, "Is it possible to minister powerfully for Christ and to know and love Christ without a remarkable charismatic experience of Christ?" Of course it is possible. Many Christians faithfully love Him and serve Him without ever really encountering Him in a deep, emotional, affectionate way. But if we can show scripturally that the latter is on offer, why settle for too little? That said, experiences may come and go, but what we must all push forward for is a "state" of Christian existence where our lives are saturated by God, utterly flooded with His Spirit. Sometimes, when I turn the bath tap on, an air pocket in the pipe causes the water to be driven out powerfully and spluttering noisily until the flow is normalized. Some may have experiences of God's Spirit like this—an initial powerful, noisy, forceful outpouring before their lives fill up. But other times, when I turn the tap on, the water immediately flows out in a gentle and measured way. Many Christians receive the fullness of the Spirit in this more measured manner. The manner in which we experience the Spirit's river of fullness flowing is not the main concern, the fact and fruit of the experience is. Throughout this book I use illustrations that often relate more to the air-pocketed, spluttering start to the bath flow, but it is the full bath that matters, not the means or moment by which the bath became full. What matters for us is not a crisis experience per se, but the fruit of a life lived in deep intimacy with and powerful ministry for Christ. What we are after is a soaking in the bath, not, as many Christians know, merely a handwashing in the basin.

John Piper incisively lays down the challenge and the glorious opportunity that is ours:

> *What we should seek (and this applies to all Christians) is that God pour His Spirit out upon us so completely that we are filled with joy, victorious over sin, and bold to witness. And the ways He brings us to that fullness are probably as varied as people are. It may come in a tumultuous experience of ecstasy and tongues. It may come through a tumultuous experience of ecstasy and no tongues. It may come through a crisis of suffering when you abandon yourself totally to God. Or it may come*

gradually through a steady diet of God's word and prayer and
fellowship and worship and service. However it comes, our first
experience of the fullness of the Spirit is only the beginning of a
life-long battle to stay filled with the Spirit.[19]

A BIBLICAL EXPECTANCY

Well, it is one thing to cite some subjective illustrations and literary allusions, but, as my friend Vaughan Roberts has rightly cautioned me, we must seek to be guided by a "biblical line of expectancy." The Scriptures are our source and norm for all doctrine and details of life with God. And so we must formulate our theology primarily from Scripture, which is where I want to take us next. But before we turn to the Bible, let me first tell a story about the distinguished professor John McIntyre and examine why this biblical line of expectancy is so important.

While preparing some lectures at Princeton on the Holy Spirit, Professor McIntyre came to the realization that the church had increasingly failed to do justice to the Bible's teaching on the subject. He wondered if the radical discontinuity between the New Testament teaching and the church's life constituted a "betrayal by the modern Church of the [New Testament] understanding of the very being of God and how he acts in the hearts of believers, in the life of the Church, and in the history of the world." Fourteen years later, when he was teaching at Edinburgh University, he revisited the biblical texts on this theme and was struck again with renewed force that, if not betrayal, there was certainly "a vast difference between the biblical and modern understanding of the nature and role of the Holy

Spirit."[20] I hope to show where the modern church has often been defective in light of what the Scriptures reveal concerning the person and work of the Spirit in the life of the Christian.

On a personal note it is because I am a conservative evangelical in my attitude to the authority and supremacy of Scripture that I am also committed to what might be termed "charismatic" theology and spirituality. Sadly some evangelicals have not been evangelical enough in looking to and following through the biblical theology of life in the Spirit. It is also true that some charismatics have not been evangelical enough in allowing Scripture to establish the norms for the nature of life in the Spirit. In this book I will explore how Scripture repeatedly promotes examples of those who sought more knowledge and experience of God, that it exhorts us to expect that there is more to know and experience of God, and that it reveals those exigencies that militate against knowing and experiencing more of God.

Barth said that we must expect more from God and act to receive this. "We ought to apply ourselves with all our strength to expect more from God … are the springs which might be flowing really flowing so abundantly?"[21]

Are you satisfied with your spiritual life to date? Do you know that unspeakable joy, that victory over sin, and that effective power for service? If your response to any of these is no, then will you seek it with me as I seek to follow the pathways, principles, and personalities of the Spirit-filled life through this book?

CHAPTER 2

EXPECT MORE

I am my beloved's and he is mine. (Song 2:16)

Christianity is a love story. It is about love lost at Eden and love restored at Calvary.

We alone out of all creation were made not merely to serve God but to love Him and be loved by Him. It was not the angels and archangels whom He made for love; He made them for ministry (Heb. 1:14), He made us for intimacy (v. 13; Eph. 2:6).

> *Wilt thou love God as He thee? Then digest*
> *My soul this wholesome meditation*
> *How God the Spirit, by Angels waited on*
> *In heaven, doth make His temple in thy breast.*[1]

Satan was filled with jealousy at the focus of God's heart and ever since has railed against us. The heart of God, the desire of

God, the greatest command of God, is not about obedience, not about worship, not about service, not about study, but about love—loving God with everything we have, even as He loves us with everything He has. But, sadly, we have often replaced love with law, intimacy with theology, delight in God with duty to God, being found with God with being sound about God. Our speech about God has the cold sterility of the scientist rather than the thrill of the poet. We have interpreted the texts, but we have sometimes failed to experience the reality behind them. The Holy Spirit today and always is calling His church back to intimacy with King Jesus.

Was there ever a time when Christ was nearer, dearer, and sweeter to you? When you longed simply to be with Him, to hear from Him, to know Him even as you were known by Him? Is there a way back to that place? Yes. The Holy Spirit, the Love between Father and Son, is sent to unite us to God in love.[2] Paul tells us that it is the role of the Spirit to shed abroad the love of God in our hearts (Rom. 5:5). The Spirit is the divine matchmaker who unites us and consummates our relationship with Christ.

REDEEMED TO BE LOVERS

The Song of Solomon is a celebration of human sexuality and intimacy in marriage. Yet it can also be understood as an allegory of God's relationship with His people,[3] a vision of the union of the Christian soul with Christ. The beloved (bride or church) is not content simply to rest on the fact that she is the bride. That would be absurd. She wants to enter into the glories and intimacies that come with being the bride. She wants to be embraced, kissed, touched, stroked, adored, known, united with her lover. And her lover wants the very same thing—to examine, to kiss, to taste, to know, and to be known. This is a book of pure passion, desire, abandonment, and even a little frustration when love cannot be consummated.

I believe this text should be far more influential in our understanding and articulation of our relationship with Christ. Charles Grandison Finney, the great early nineteenth-century revivalist, recalled in his memoirs how, in the latter part of his ministry, he knew deep times of intimacy with Christ by the Spirit. He says, "The language of the Song of Solomon was as natural to me as my breath."[4] I too have often been compelled by the Spirit to learn to pray for the sense of intimacy with Christ, urgency for Christ, and ecstasy with Christ that the beloved has with her lover. Yet for many, to think and speak in such intimate terms about their relationship with Christ would seem utterly alien.

We need to kindle that flame of passion for Him. We need to find the kisses of His mouth more delightful than wine (Song 1:2). We need to be taken to His banquet hall and know that His banner over us is love (2:4). We need to lie on our beds all night looking and longing for His love (3:1). We need to hear Him speak words of love over us, to know His thoughts for us (4:1f.). We need to hear Him knock on the door and bid us open to Him (5:2). We need to arise to Him and be willing to go out into the night after Him, no matter what obstacle stands in our way (5:6f.). We need to show to the world that "I am my beloved's and he is mine" (6:3), and we need to know His constant refrain over us, "My love, my dove, you are beautiful" (6:4, 9–10). We need to desire the One who desires us (7:10) and take Him to that secret place where we give Him our love (7:12b). We need to know and show Him love that "flashes like fire" (8:6). This love between lovers, which waters cannot quench, which floods cannot drown, which offers cannot tempt away (8:7)—this is the love that must mark our marriage to Christ.

Jesus is not simply our Redeemer, but our Lover. Love redeemed us to be lovers. Redemption is not just from sin, death, and hell, but to and for blazing intimacy with Jesus. Too often we have reduced the work of Christ to some metaphysical, judicial exchange and missed the fact that it is a marriage—not of convenience (escaping hell), but of consuming, consummating love (entering heaven). We have developed and dissected our theories of atonement, but have we learned to love and be loved by Christ the Lover? How different our walk with Christ, our witness to Christ, our work for Christ, would be if we knew ourselves truly loved and desired by Christ. Even as some marriages become stale and dutiful, losing their passion, their intimacy, their delight, their tenderness, so too may our relationship with our Lord grow dim.

The prophets repeatedly voiced the tragic cries from God's heart, revealing His crushing privation at Israel's dissipated love for Him. "I remember the devotion of your youth, your love as a bride" (Jer. 2:2). Having once made herself ready for her lover, "Can a virgin forget her adornments or a bride her attire? Yet My people have forgotten Me …" (v. 32). God, the great Lover, "spread the corner of [His] garment over us" (a sexual metaphor), vowed to us, washed us, anointed us, clothed us, adorned us, and graced us (Ezek. 16:8f.), and although we may not have abandoned God as Israel did, perhaps, like the Ephesian church, we have forsaken or fallen from that first love (Rev. 2:4).

Let me refer briefly to three medieval mystics who all drank deeply of the life in the Spirit and who were all captivated by the allegorical story in Song of Solomon of the believer's union with Christ.

Song of Solomon 1:2 says, "Let him kiss me with the kisses of his mouth" (NIV). The great twelfth-century Christian mystic Bernard of Clairvaux, reflecting on this verse, said, "The Kiss of God is the gift of the Holy Spirit."[5] Bernard understood the Holy Spirit in terms of the kiss of love between the Father and the Son. This Holy Spirit given to us by Christ is God's kiss of love to us. By that same Spirit, in a cyclic movement, we kiss God in response. We are only able to love God with our whole strength, as He commands, when our soul has experienced the fullness of the Spirit.[6]

William of St. Thierry, reflecting on the Song of Solomon, also saw this experience by the Spirit as an invasion of love that brought "an abundance of grace to the point of positive and palpable experience of something of God, suddenly, in a new way, something comes within the grasp of the sense of enlightened love which exceeds the reach of any bodily sense, the consideration of reason and all understanding, except the understanding of enlightened love."[7] Thierry pointedly asks us whether love is one thing and the feeling of love another. For him the answer must be emphatically no.

Richard Rolle was an Oxford academic and mystic. For Rolle the experience of God was the burning fire of love by the Spirit. He was keenly aware that "not everyone who follows [Jesus'] commands follows his advice and not everyone who acts by his advice is filled with the sweetness of his love and feels the fire burning in his heart."[8] Rolle believed there were three levels of loving Christ—a mere love that obeys His commands, a love whose heart is constantly fixed on Jesus, and a love that sets you on fire and all who touch you feel the heat of it. This love, says Rolle, is indescribable:

> *Then your soul is loving Jesus, thinking Jesus, desiring Jesus, breathing only in its desire for him, singing to him, catching fire for him, resting in him. Then your thought turns into song and into harmony. Then you feel compelled to sing the psalms which previously you recited ... Then death will seem to you sweeter than honey, because then you are most certain to see him whom you love ... then you can say I am sleeping, but my heart is awake.*[9]

This condition Rolle calls "languishing in love," literally dissipating through exhaustion in love.

Do you not long to find that place, by God's grace, where you love Christ so dearly that you want nothing else but to be united with Him? Does your soul not long after God as the deer pants for water? Does your deep not cry to His deep in the roar of His waterfall (Ps. 42:1, 7)? If not, pray for the longing to long. I long for that kiss of the Lover. No ordinary kiss, no titillating smack on the lips, but something to take my breath away. That lingering, loving intimacy whereby I know and am known. Where lovers are joined, become one, share the same space, breath, moment.

At the first kiss I felt
Something melt inside me
That hurt in an exquisite way
All my longings, all my dreams, and sweet anguish,
All the secrets that slept deep within me came awake,
Everything was transformed and enchanted
And made sense.[10]

The great Puritan Richard Sibbes also spoke of the gift of the seal of the Spirit (Eph. 1:14) in intimate terms: "spiritual ravishings which are the very beginning of heaven …" and the Christian "is in heaven before his time" having an assurance which is "a sweet kiss of the soul."[11] Listen to the Puritan Samuel Rutherford, imprisoned for his faith, yet enraptured with Christ:

to see and smell and touch and kiss that fair field-flower, that evergreen Tree of life!… Christ, Christ, nothing but Christ can cool our love's burning languor. O thirsty Love! Wilt thou set Christ, the well of life to thy head and drink thy fill? Drink and spare not; drink love, and be drunken with Christ. Nay alas! The distance between us and Christ is death; Oh, if we were clasped in each other's arms.[12]

We must learn to yearn for that renewing of the Holy Spirit, so that we might be renewed in our love for our Savior. That is what Jude calls us to when he says, "pray in the Holy Spirit. Keep yourselves in God's love …" (vv. 20–21 NIV). That is why Paul prays for the Ephesians (3:14–19 NIV) that they might be inwardly strengthened with power by the Spirit, who grounds them in love, enabling them "to grasp how wide and long and high and deep is the love of Christ, and to know this love that surpasses knowledge—that you may be filled to the measure of all the fullness of God." But, dear God, they resisted Paul's prayers and later this Ephesian church was rebuked for having "forsaken their first love" (Rev. 2:4).

May that never be true of us. May we, by God's Spirit, know, grow, and show that love of God that unites us with Christ. God wants our kiss in return. The most common term for "worship" in the New Testament is *proskuneo*, a conjunction of two terms that literally means to come before and kiss. The Lord would say to us, "Will you kiss Me with the kisses of your lips?"

One of the genuine marks of any Holy Spirit renewal is to cause us to fall in love again with Christ. The Spirit blows on the dying embers of our passion and fans them to flame. Once again we are like dizzy teenagers, consumed with passion for our Savior, wanting nothing else than to give ourselves to Him, unable to think or speak of anything but Christ in all His glory. In the time of the great outpouring of God's Spirit in New England under the ministry of Jonathan Edwards, Edwards would often exhort his listeners to see themselves as virgins preparing for Christ the bridegroom. He spoke in highly sensual terms of our being ravished by the love of Christ and being filled with the Spirit.[13] In a famous account Edwards' wife Sarah recalls a remarkable personal encounter with Christ by the Spirit in which for several hours she lay, unable to move, on her bed. She recalls it as:

> *the sweetest night I ever had in my life … all night I continued*
> *in a constant, clear, and lively sense of the heavenly sweetness of*

Christ's excellent love, of his nearness and dearness to me, and
my dearness to him … I seemed to myself to perceive a glow
of divine love come down from the heart of Christ … At the
same time my heart and soul all flowed out in love to Christ
so that there seemed to be a constant flowing and re-flowing of
heavenly love.[14]

And what was the fruit of such an experience, if the sheer joy and ecstasy of loving and being loved by Christ is not enough? This woman became a great source of inspiration to many to pursue more of God and to live more for God. She lived a life ever after that was deeply consecrated and submitted to Jesus, and she was delivered from the depression that had dogged her for many years.[15]

A young lawyer named Charles Finney, the outstanding evangelist of the early nineteenth century, spoke of the experience of God by the Holy Spirit that catapulted him into ministry. As he sat at his office desk, the Holy Spirit descended on him as "waves and waves of liquid love." He wrote, "No words can express the wonderful love that was shed abroad in my heart. I wept aloud with joy and love … I literally bellowed out the unutterable gushings of my heart."[16]

Whatever we may call this encounter, I want it. Don't you? And I don't just want it once, but in ever-increasing measure, pressed down and running over. I need an immersion in the love of God and a rekindling with love for God. To quote the fifteenth-century medieval mystic Bianco of Siena, "Come down O love divine, enter this soul of mine, and visit it with thine own ardour glowing."

A THIRST QUENCHED

In John 4 we read of an extraordinary encounter that Jesus had with a Samaritan woman with an eyebrow-raising past.

Engaging her in conversation as she draws up the water from the well, He asks her for a drink. She is somewhat taken aback, as it was so unusual for a Jew to talk with a Samaritan, let alone a Jewish rabbi with a Samaritan woman. Having accepted a drink of water from her, Jesus immediately offers her something in return: He promises her that whoever drinks of the water He gives "will never thirst again," and that this water will well up to eternal life (John 4:14).

We see Jesus make a similar promise later (John 7:37f.) in a powerfully prophetic context. On each of the seven days of the Feast of Booths, a priest would draw water from the pool of Siloam in a golden flagon and bring it in procession to the temple amid the exultant crowds and the sound of trumpets. There the water was poured into a bowl that fed through a tube to the base of the altar. This symbolic act was both a thanksgiving to God for the provision of water and a petition for rain the following year. Certain rabbis and the Jerusalem Talmud suggest that during this act, the crowds sang the words of Isaiah 12:3, "With joy you shall draw water out of the wells of salvation," and they understood this act to be prophetic of the anticipated pouring out of the Holy Spirit.[17] What is most significant in light of this is that as the priests pour out the water, the crowds watch and pray and anticipate. Christ commandeers this prophetic event and directs it to Himself as the One who will ultimately give that which satisfies: He brings the Holy Spirit.

Here He extends an invitation not just to one woman, but to a crowd of people at the temple, and proffers this promise: To any who thirst, if they believe in Him and come to Him, they might drink and satiate their thirst, and out of them[18] would flow rivers of living water. If we put the two texts from the Samaritan well and the Jerusalem temple together—and I hope you will agree that they fit both semantically and thematically—Jesus makes a twofold promise. If we believe in Him and come to Him, and drink of the Holy Spirit He offers, we will never thirst again and we will receive eternal life.

Now it seems to me that much of our evangelical preaching and much of our evangelical experience appropriates only four-fifths of Christ's promise. We believe and come to Jesus and receive the Holy Spirit and are assured of eternal life. But are we satisfied? I confess I'm not. And my sense is that many Christians would agree with me. Of course we are far more satisfied than we were before we came and believed in Christ, primarily because we have assurance that our sins are forgiven and our eternal life in heaven is secure. And I am not discontent with this at all. Such grace, such glory is beyond imagining. The world has nothing to match it. However, here and now I confess that I still thirst, and I suspect many other Christians do too. I am certain I will not thirst in heaven, and I am not expecting heaven now, but a foretaste of it. Is not this temporal satisfaction part of the promise of Christ by the Holy Spirit today? Perhaps this thirst is why we are so often lured away by the illusory offer of satisfaction from the shipwrecking Sirens of this world: career, success, wealth, possessions, sex, and so on.

What do I make of this? Is my exegesis wrong and resulting in an expectation that is wrong? Maybe the "never thirsting" (John

4:14) is eschatologically focused; that is, we will never thirst again once we get to heaven. That is certainly true, and yet the promise never to thirst again, the invitation to believe, to come now and drink and by implication be satisfied, is surely not all posited in the future. Jesus does not seem to be saying, "You who thirst, come, believe, drink of Me, and I will give you a river of the Holy Spirit, and one day, when you get to heaven, you will have eternal life and never thirst again—oh, but until then, expect to thirst." That does not seem to fit the obvious meaning of the texts. There is undeniably a time gap between Christ's promise and His listeners' appropriation, but they will not have to wait until they get to heaven—they need only wait for Christ to get to heaven and release heaven to them, at Pentecost. "By this He meant the Holy Spirit, whom those who believed in Him were to receive, for as yet the Spirit had not been given as Jesus had not been glorified" (7:39). But He is there now, and the promised Spirit of satisfaction has been released, and yet I still thirst! What does this mean? The twofold promise of eternal life and satisfaction appears to be conditioned by a threefold response: believe, come, drink. I do believe in Christ, absolutely. But do I come? Sometimes. Do I drink? Sometimes. And here perhaps is the key. I experience a partial appropriation because of a partial response. "There is a river whose streams make glad the city of God" (Ps. 46:4 NIV)—that river of the Holy Spirit, opened up for us through Christ at Calvary. But have we stopped it up, or diverted it, or avoided it?

In the French film *Jean de Florette,* adapted from the book by Marcel Pagnol, the story is told of a hunchback who inherits a farm. When he arrives there, he seeks to make the farm successful and works hard day and night, expending all his energy and efforts, all his finances and investing in all the latest farming techniques to make it viable. But despite his painstaking, backbreaking efforts, his crops begin to wither and his animals begin to die, because there is no water. The naturally fed artesian well dries up due to the lack of rain. Daily he crosses the mountains with his donkey, laden down with pots and pans and churns, to collect water from another running stream—but he cannot collect enough and soon everything dies. Eventually, in desperation, he turns to dowsing and, thinking he has found water underground, he uses explosives to unearth it, only to be mortally wounded by a falling rock. On his deathbed Jean admits, "I failed to see that water was the one problem …" The tragedy of this dark story is that there was a river running the whole time under his land, but it had been stopped up by wicked men who sought his downfall in order to rob him of his inheritance.

Often that river of God's Spirit is blocked up or diverted from flowing to and through our lives bringing renewal, life, growth, and harvest (Gen. 26:18f.). It is diverted by our own sin, by the world, the flesh, and the Devil. Some of us have struggled and strained, looking here, there, and everywhere for water to irrigate our lives, but we have never found enough. The river of God is more than enough. And it is not somewhere over the mountain, but within us. We need only look to Christ and His power to remove the rubble—the accumulation of sin, demonic bondage, enemy footholds, resentments, bitterness, worldly affections, faithlessness, lack of spiritual desire—and the Spirit will rush forward, turning barrenness to beauty, desert into oasis, struggle into satisfaction.[19] Jesus Himself went to the cross and declared, "I thirst" (John 19:28), so that we might never have to say the same again.

In a sermon on John 7:38, C. H. Spurgeon said these remarkable prophetic words:

> *Ask God to make you all that the Spirit of God can make you, not only a satisfied believer who has drunk for himself, but a useful believer who overflows the neighbourhood with blessing … [seeing some visitors in his church he directed his words to them] what a blessing it would be if they went back to their respective churches overflowing; for there are numbers of churches that need flooding; they are dry as a barn floor, and little dew ever falls on them. Oh that they might be flooded … What a wonderful thing a flood is … Oh for a flood of grace! The Lord send to all our churches a great springtide … so may it be, may all who hear me this day get your share of the streams. Oh that the Lord may now fill you and send you home bearing a flood of grace … !*[20]

Some have tapped into this satiating river of the Holy Spirit. Have you? In 1735 a remarkable evangelist named Howell Harris, who was later used powerfully to bring a revival across Wales, met God and drank deeply from this river of life. His experience combines many of the experiences associated with the deep work of the Holy Spirit: assurance, joy, love, and not least a drinking from that river that quenches thirst. Often referring back to that experience, he recalled:

I felt suddenly my heart melting within me like wax before the fire with love to God my saviour, and felt not only love, peace etc., but longing to be dissolved and to be with Christ; then was a cry in my inmost soul which I was totally unacquainted with before "Abba, Father! Abba, Father!" I could not help calling God my father. I knew that I was his child and that he loved me and heard me. My soul being filled and satiated, crying "'tis enough, I am satisfied. Give me strength and I will follow thee through water and fire." I could say I was happy indeed! There was in me a well of water, springing up to everlasting life, John 4:14.[21]

Can you imagine being so saturated with the presence of God's Holy Spirit that you felt you could take no more and had to ask God to stop pouring, saying, "'Tis enough"? Finney, when filled by the Holy Spirit in the love of God, cried, "Lord, I cannot bear any more!" Moody, when filled with the Spirit, said, "I had to ask Him to stay His hand." For them, filled with the Holy Spirit really meant filled.

FILLED MEANS FILLED

All afternoon, as I sat trying to watch sports on TV, my son Joel was blowing up balloons acquired at some party. That week his lungs had reached sufficient strength to break the initial resistance of the rubber and begin to inflate the balloon. He would blow them up and then, rather than tie them off, would let them go so that they made unmentionable noises while spinning round the living room. Proud of his lung capacity, he would hold up a balloon and say to me, "There, Dad, that's full." I would take it from him, careful to pinch the nozzle to avoid any air leaking out, and was able to blow another few breaths of air into it. He had inflated it, but he had not completely filled it. One should not push an analogy too far, but suffice it to say that Christians, like balloons, come in all different shapes and sizes, with varying capacities for air—varying anointings, giftings, callings. We must resist the idea that everyone's Spirit-filled life is the same—they are manifestly not, as we see from 1 Corinthians 12. Joel believed the balloon was full, but I knew there was room for more. Many of us may consider ourselves full, but God may have more to put in us. The main application is that we must offer ourselves constantly to the Lord to be filled and refilled, so that we reach the fullness of our individual capacity.

In Scripture the word *filled* is a spatial term depicting the filling or abundance of things with particular objects—for example, land "overrun" with idols, the banks of the Jordan "brimming" with water, land "densely populated" with people, the temple "wall to wall" with the glory of the Lord. In Greek the word *plerou*, from which we get our word *plethora*, was used of a ship's sail "billowing" with wind, a jar brimming with liquid, a fragrance filling a room, hills "covered" in trees, time reaching its completion, possession by something or by emotions. When the Bible speaks of being filled with the Holy Spirit, it is saying that one is consumed, taken over, impregnated, saturated, complete, and replete with God's presence and power. To be filled with the Holy Spirit leaves no room to be filled with anything else.[22]

The word for the Holy Spirit in the Bible can equally be translated breath/wind/spirit in both the Old Testament—Hebrew *ruach*—and the New Testament—Greek *pneuma*. As with water, the other key metaphor used to describe the person of the Spirit, the breath/wind/spirit metaphor is naturally understood in terms of space, quantity, volume, and measure, and throughout the Scriptures we meet men and women "measurably" or "quantitatively" filled with this Holy Spirit, this life-empowering breath of God, this divine river. Let's look at some of the examples of being "filled" from the Old Testament to the New.

Bezalel was filled with God's Spirit and the ability and intelligence of all craftsmanship to help design all the utensils and furnishings for God's holy tabernacle (Ex. 31:2f.; 35:30). Joshua was filled with the Spirit of God and empowered to defeat Israel's enemies and lead them into the Promised Land (Deut. 34:9). John the Baptist was filled with the Holy Spirit from birth, set apart, and anointed to be the forerunner of Christ (Luke 1:15). His mother, Elizabeth, was filled with the Spirit when she saw Mary pregnant with Jesus, and she prophesied blessing, revelation, and encouragement over our Lord's mother (vv. 41f.). Similarly her husband, Zechariah, John's father, was filled with the Holy Spirit and prophesied concerning his son and his part in the salvation history of God (vv. 67f.).

In Acts 2:2 we read that on the day of Pentecost the whole house was filled with the mighty wind (*pneuma*) of God that separated and rested on each of those gathered in prayer. They were all filled with the Spirit (v. 4) and spoke in tongues, prophesying the wonders of God. Later, before the Sanhedrin, Peter is again[23] filled with the Holy Spirit and proclaims Christ before his accusers. Returning from arrest, he goes to a prayer meeting, the room is shaken, and, as with the recent Pentecost, "they were all filled with the Holy Spirit and spoke the word of God boldly" (Acts 4:31 NIV).

Later, when the church seeks people to help with the menial task of waiting on tables, they look for those who are "filled with the Holy Spirit" (Acts 6:3). Stephen, a man filled with faith and the Spirit (6:5), filled with grace and power for signs and wonders (v. 8), is one of those chosen. Brought before the Sanhedrin, he preaches against their hard hearts and, full of the Holy Spirit, he has a vision of the glory of God and Christ standing at God's right hand.[24] When he declares this to his enraged listeners, they stone him to death, and this Spirit-filled man, like his Savior, forgives them with his last breath.

In Acts 9:17, when Ananias lays hands on Saul, he receives the Spirit and is healed of his blindness. His remarkable ministry of preaching Christ begins immediately. In Acts 11:24 we meet Barnabas, an apostle in Antioch, who is "full of faith and the Holy Spirit," and whose ministry brings a great number to Christ. He teams up with Paul, and the two of them go to Cyprus (13:4f.), where a demonic magician named Elymas resists them. Paul, filled with the Holy Spirit (again), prophesies against this enemy of the gospel, who is instantly struck blind. In Acts 13:52 the ministry of Paul and Barnabas in Antioch results in the disciples being "filled with the Holy Spirit and joy."

Paul's last word is not the last word! In the letter to the Romans, probably the only non-context-specific troubleshooting Pauline letter, but his most systematic presentation of gospel doctrine, Paul brackets his letter with an *inclusio* of more. Paul both begins and draws his letter to a close by anticipating a visit to the Romans that he hopes will be a visitation from God through an apostolic impartation. "I long to see you, that I may impart some spiritual gift to you that you may be established …" (Rom. 1:11). "I know that when I come to you, I will come in the fullness of the blessing of Christ" (15:29). Doctrine in the form of his letter to them is not enough. Paul intends to come in the fullness of the Spirit to impart to them an additional spiritual blessing, so that they might attain the fullness, not simply of Bible knowledge but of spiritual experience.

So what does it mean to be filled with the Holy Spirit? What may we deduce from all these references? What are the predicates attached to this filling with the Holy Spirit?

- Being filled with the Holy Spirit elicits creative gifts, leadership gifts, wisdom, prophetic utterances, revelation of God's purposes, praise, boldness and authority in speech, faith, power to perform signs and wonders, grace, personal healing, authority, attractive drawing people to Christ, conquering confrontation with the powers of darkness, and joy.

- The coming of the Spirit may be associated with external, observable, tangible phenomena like the sounds of mighty wind or the shaking of rooms.

- Filling with the Spirit is repeatable, occurring at least three times for Peter, at least twice with Paul, and at least twice for the Pentecost Christians in Acts 2 and 4.

- A person full of the Spirit is clearly distinguishable from one who is not, thus enabling the selection of deacons known to be Spirit filled.

- A Spirit-filled life does not preclude one from suffering; on the contrary, it may invite persecution, yet it also produces grace to forgive one's persecutors.
- Being filled with the Spirit may lead to a notable public ministry, as it did with Paul or Stephen, but equally it may not, as with the majority at Pentecost.
- Being filled with the Spirit comes at times of intercession, affliction, or separation for ministry.
- In the New Testament, being filled with the Holy Spirit is always associated with a greater revelation from, praise to, proclamation of, and life lived for Jesus Christ.

This is just some of the evidence presented by the Scriptures for the Spirit-filled life. What is the evidence in you?

In Ephesians 5:18, Paul says, "Do not get drunk on wine, which leads to debauchery. Instead, be filled with the Spirit" (NIV). Paul here is influenced by Jewish tradition, which made a comparison between being drunk and being possessed by God—in both states one is under the influence, coming under the control of an external power.[25] It is not a coincidence that strong liquors are called "spirits." Paul is not concerned with the physical phenomena attached to the states of being drunk on alcohol or filled with the Spirit—be that flushed, falling, or foolish. His concern is to encourage every believer to be under the influence of and possessed by God—divinely intoxicated. One often hears it said of alcoholics that they are "old soaks." Paul wants us to be "God soaked."

That Paul can even make this command to be filled implies that many believers are not. It is not to deny that they have the Holy Spirit, but simply to say that they could have more—or that the Spirit could have more of them. This verse is also the linchpin of a long ethical section running from Ephesians 4:17 to 6:20. Paul is saying that if we are to live a life marked by personal holiness and mutual love, and if we are to fight and stand against the demonic principalities and powers, we must be filled with the Spirit. This is not a matter of a spiritual frisson, but of authentic Christian living. The Methodist divine Samuel Chadwick said, "A ministry that is college trained but not Spirit filled works no miracles."[26] Paul wants the church to be Spirit filled, because only then can she fulfill her destiny.

We must note the important structure of Paul's command. First comes the imperative—this is not an optional extra for the Christian life, but an order with a responsibility placed on us to be filled. Second comes the passive—it is not something we do to or for ourselves, but something that is done to us. We receive, we cannot fill ourselves, we can only seek and submit to being filled. Third comes the iterative—this experience is to be a constantly repeated one, indeed a continual state for the believer. Presumably this Spirit-filled state can be lost, or perhaps never found, by disobedience, ignorance, or indifference.

Paul does not merely tell them what they need. Day and night he is fervent in prayer for them to receive this. In Ephesians 3:19 we see him constantly petitioning God that the Ephesian church may be "filled with all the fullness of God." In Colossians 1:19 we read that Jesus is the fullness of God. Paul is praying that God, in Christ, by the Spirit, may be totally presented in, to, and through them; that the fullness of God, His characteristics of power, glory, grace, and love, may mark them. But it does not yet, and so Paul prays on. As one commentator says, "There is a goal which has not yet been attained and the goal is to be filled with what distinguishes God."[27]

WHAT ARE YOU FILLED WITH?

If Acts is where we most see men and women described as filled with the Holy Spirit, it also offers another picture of men and women filled with unholy spirits. Ananias and Sapphira allowed Satan to fill their hearts with greed and deceit (5:3). The high priest and his leaders were filled with jealousy at the miraculous ministry of the apostles and had them arrested (v. 17). Again the Jews in Antioch were filled with jealousy at the crowds drawn by Paul and Barnabas, and they challenged and reviled them (13:45). The whole city of Ephesus, which had embraced the apostolic ministry of Paul, was suddenly filled with confusion by Demetrius' vehement verbal opposition (19:29). If we are to be filled with the Holy Spirit, we must not grieve the Holy Spirit (Eph. 4:30), and we must repent, renounce, and remove anything else that would fill our lives and crowd out the Holy Spirit—lust, pride, ambition, envy, greed, resentment, bitterness, unforgiveness, self-pity, a critical spirit. He is the Holy Spirit, and He cannot fill what is defiled. Repentance precedes reception of the Spirit (Acts 2:38).

The godly Victorian minister and missionary Andrew Murray suggested four practical and verbal steps we must take to being filled by God's Spirit:[28]

> *Step 1—Say "I must be filled"—knowing that God commands it and you need it.*

Step 2—Say "I may be filled"—believing that it is God's promise to all believers.

Step 3—Say "I should be filled"—willing to surrender all for that pearl of great price.

Step 4—Say "I shall be filled"—claiming the promised gift of God, purchased by Christ.

But if you desire to be filled with the Holy Spirit, let me warn you that you have a battle on your hands. As we saw in our study of Scripture, a Spirit-filled Christian is an awesome weapon in the hands of God for the establishment of God's rule and reign.

A. W. Tozer spoke with prophetic incision when he said:

Satan has opposed the doctrine of the Spirit filled life about as bitterly as any doctrine there is. He has confused it, opposed it, and surrounded it with false notions and fears. He has blocked every effort of the Church of Christ to receive from the Father the divine and blood bought patrimony. The Church has tragically neglected this great liberating truth that there is now, for the child of God, a full and wonderful and completely satisfying anointing with the Holy Spirit. The Spirit filled life is not a special deluxe edition of Christianity. It is part and parcel of the total plan of God for his people.[29]

CHAPTER 3

MAY DAY

While walking in the meadows of Christ Church College discussing theology with a fellow minister, I was asked the question, "On what basis can the charismatics say there is more to be had of the Holy Spirit?" Similar to the man who accused me of teaching false doctrine, many wonder: How can the Spirit come when we have Him already? How can we have more when we already have Him "in person," not piecemeal, in our lives? Some evangelicals are rightly concerned that talk of more appears to imply an addition or distinction from the gospel. They worry that it implies a development from and even a deficiency in the cross. May God deal with us, be it ever so severely, if we ever seek to devalue the glorious cross. That is by no means what this is all about. The "more" is merely an appropriation by us through the application of the Spirit of what was achieved by Christ at Calvary. We have everything in Christ. There is no more to be given, but there is more to be taken. My understanding is that to ask for more is not to undermine, but to mine the finished work of Calvary. Some have sidestepped this by saying, "It's not more of the Spirit we should ask for, but more of ourselves we should give the Spirit." This, of course, is true—but I still believe it is appropriate to speak in terms of having more of the Holy Spirit. Think about the promise of Jesus: that if we, though we are evil, know how to give good gifts, "how much more" will the Father give the Spirit to those who ask (Luke 11:13).

It may be helpful to imagine this as another way to grow in Christ, to which few would object. Look at Christians throughout the ages who, out of spiritual hunger and desire, experienced a greater, deeper encounter and anointing. Or the reality of honest Christians who know that they have not allowed God to become a significant or dominant feature in their speech, acts, and thoughts.

While the Holy Spirit is a person in our lives, it is possible to live like strangers in the same house. Has He been with us this long and still we do not know Him (John 14:9)? Whether through ignorance, willful disobedience, or indifference, we can fail to allow Him to manifest His character and power in and through us. He resides in us, His temple, but we may not always be led by Him, listening to Him, loving Him, or letting Him live through us. Instead we lock Him out of places; we limit the time given to Him and the reception of all He brings. The Holy Spirit does not want to be a marble statue at the entrance to our souls—He wants to fill every room, He wants to articulate Himself, and He wants to distribute all His gifts to and through us. When I pray, "Come, Holy Spirit," or ask for more, I am not thinking of an external visitation, but an internal total occupation and expression of the Spirit.

In fact, although the terms used in Scripture reflect the idea of quantity or being filled, they can also be understood as an intensification of that presence. For instance, Moses was not content with the accompanying presence of God, nor even with the audible voice and dialogue with God. Instead he petitioned Him for a personal mani-festation of His glory (Ex. 33:18). Martyn Lloyd-Jones in his chapter "Burden for Revival" describes Moses' encounter with God.

> *Moses made a request, God said, "Yes."*
> *"More," said Moses.*
> *"Right," said God.*
> *"More," said Moses.*[1]

MAY I? YOU MAY!

That day in Christ Church meadows, I answered my colleague with what I think is the key in this whole debate, and it comes down to grammar: Paul's prayers for more for the church is in the subjunctive mood. If you think back to your school days, you may recall that the subjunctive is used to express wishes, desires, or hopes that have not yet come to pass. We see Paul pray in this way notably in Ephesians 1:15f., but not exclusively. We also see this prayer in the subjunctive in Ephesians 3:16 and 18, and strikingly in Colossians 1:9, which I want to explore as a key text on the theme of "more." Here we see Paul pray that the Colossians "may be filled with," to which he attaches several attributes, all significantly prefaced by superlatives (in Greek, twice *epi*, meaning "full"; twice *pase*; twice *pasan*; once *panti*, meaning "all/ every"):

> *… that you may be filled with the full knowledge of God's will, through all spiritual wisdom and understanding, that you may lead lives worthy of the Lord, fully pleasing Him, as you bear*

fruit in every good work, and growing in the full knowledge of
God with all power, empowered according to the might of His
glory with all endurance, longsuffering with joy …

Clearly there was more.

The placing of Paul's prayer for more in Ephesians 1 is structurally significant. Before looking forward in prayer, Paul looks back in praise. Before he tells them what they may have, he reminds them (in vv. 3–14) what they already have. These glorious gifts are referred to in the past tense, as something that has already been accomplished, achieved, and implemented in their lives. Thus, Paul tells them, they have been blessed in Christ with every spiritual blessing in the heavenly places (v. 3), chosen before the foundation of the world (v. 4), predestined to be adopted (v. 5), blessed in the Beloved (v. 6), redeemed through the blood (v. 7), lavished with grace (v. 8), had the mystery of His will made known to them (v. 9), received an inheritance, having been predestined (v. 11), and sealed with the Holy Spirit who guarantees their inheritance (vv. 13f.). And all this only in Christ (vv. 4, 6–7, 9–11, 13); all this to his praise and glory (vv. 6, 12, 14).

Wow. I could stop right there and spend the rest of my life lost in wonder, love, praise, and service to God for such grace lavished upon us, unworthy, wretched sinners, in this glorious gospel. I could—but Paul does not. Paul keeps pressing on for more. This "more," however, is not additional to or distinct from God's actions in verses 3–14, but flows out of what has already happened. The bridge of verse 15 makes this clear: "for this reason" (in light of and all that has already been given us in Christ), let us fully avail ourselves now. The "more" is only on the basis of what went before.

Between verses 14 and 15 there is a space in many Bible versions (e.g., GNB, NIV, ESV, NKJV), indicating a substantive thematic change. Sadly, this is a gap into which many Christians fall, living their lives from Ephesians 1:3–14, but never advancing beyond that. Would Paul pray for "more" if we did not need more, or if Christ did not want to give us more, or if there was no more? This is not a matter of spiritual indulgence, but kingdom significance. The gifted nineteenth-century preacher and evangelist A. J. Gordon once remarked, "Why should we be satisfied with 'the forgiveness of sins according to the riches of his grace' (Eph. 1:7), when the Lord would grant us also 'according to the riches of his glory, to be strengthened with might by his Spirit in the inner man' (Eph. 3:16)?"[2]

Let's cross this gap, and see what can be deduced after verse 14, but based on what he has said prior.

First, the "more" is centered on Christ. The whole prayer for "more" is framed by Jesus. He is the basis of the more (v. 15), He is the focus of the more, He is the content of the more. Paul's prayer for more ends with his praise to Christ (vv. 20–22).

Second, the "more" is claimed in prayer. In verse 17, Paul keeps praying that God may give them the Spirit of wisdom and revelation; in verse 18 Paul prays that the eyes of their hearts may be opened. Prayer is the pathway to the provisions God has laid up for us.

Third, "more" is conveyed by the Spirit. In verse 17b, Paul's prayer is for the Spirit of wisdom and understanding that will enable them to know God fully. In particular he prays that they may know the power that raised Jesus from the dead (v. 20), which is the Holy Spirit (see Rom. 1:4). They already possess the seal of the Spirit (vv. 13f.), and now Paul prays for the power of the Spirit.

Fourth, "more" is clearly for all. This is addressed to the saints at Ephesus (1:1), so this prayer is not simply for the leadership, but for all the membership. This is not some pseudo-Gnostic elite experience for the initiated. This is the birthright of every believer. Christ does not want a few anointed individuals; He wants an anointed church. Paul prays for more for the Ephesians, because they don't have it all yet. See what he says in 1:16f.:

> *I have not ceased praying for you, remembering you in my prayers, that the God of our Lord Jesus Christ may give you [aorist subjunctive* didomi*] three things: (1) the Spirit of wisdom and revelation to fully know [*epignosei*] Him; (2) having the eyes of your hearts enlightened that you may know what is the hope to which He has called you, the riches of His glorious inheritance in the saints; and (3) the immeasurable greatness of His power for us who believe.*

Paul prays for three things, mediated by the Spirit: a greater knowledge of God, a greater knowledge of what is ours in Christ, and a greater operation of the resurrection power. I'd like to look at these three things in greater detail.

KNOWING GOD

... the Spirit of wisdom and revelation to fully know Him ...

These Ephesians have the gospel, and they have the Old Testament Scriptures, and perhaps one or two apostolic inspired letters. Is this what Paul is directing them to? A greater knowledge deduced from these? Perhaps, but only partially. Paul's scriptural exhortation points to something beyond the scriptural exhortation! His prayer is that the Spirit would so work in the church that they might say with Job, "I had heard of You by the hearing of the ear, but now my eye sees You" (Job 42:5).

The knowledge of God comes through the person of Christ. Jesus told His disciples that, if they had seen Him, they had seen the Father (John 14:9). But that revelation is historically located two thousand years ago in Israel, and now Christ is seated in heaven, and between both there is fixed a great gulf. How can we today, two thousand years and several thousand miles removed, access that revelation? Calvin said that it was "the Spirit who truly unites what is separated by space" (Institutes 4.17.10). We have the Scriptures, which are an accurate, divinely inspired, human record of and response to that revelation. From this we can deduce principles and draw pictures as to that revelation. But do we also need that revelation to be revelation to us personally? I need the "outward" Word of God to become the "inward" Word of God to me. How? By faith and by the work of the Spirit. I need the Spirit to illumine to me what He inspired through them. Calvin saw this clearly when he spoke of the *testimonium internum Spiritus Sancti*—the internal witness of the Holy Spirit, who alone can authenticate His Word.

Without the revealing activity of the Spirit, as the Protestant theologian Jean Bosc says, "The Word alone always runs the risk of incurring a kind of sclerosis at our hands. Christ imprisoned in our neat formulas can become an abstract dogma, the Bible can become a dead letter."[3]

Jesus said that the Spirit would guide us into all truth, teach us things that are to come, and glorify Christ by taking what is His and declaring it to us (John 16:13). Paul says that the Spirit searches the deep things of God, giving us understanding of them, which we in turn impart by the Spirit (1 Cor. 2:10–13).

- The Bible states that Jesus is Lord, but the Spirit makes that real to me (1 Cor. 12:3).
- The Bible states that God is Father, but the Spirit makes that real to me (Rom. 8:15).
- The Bible states that God is glorious, but the Spirit makes that real to me (2 Cor. 3:10f.).
- The Bible states that God is love, but the Spirit makes that real to me (Eph. 3:16f.).

In 1654 the French mathematician and philosopher Blaise Pascal recorded a revelation he had by the Holy Spirit that made the God of Scripture real to him. He wrote it on a piece of parchment and sewed it into his doublet, next to his heart, where it stayed until it was found on him at his death. It read:

Fire
God of Abraham, God of Isaac, God of Jacob (Ex. 6:3).

Not of the philosophers and scientists
Certitude, certitude. Feeling. Joy. Peace.
My God and your God (John 20:17).

You shall be my God (Ruth 1:16).[4]

Likewise, on a voyage to America where he precipitated a revival, George Whitefield knew a remarkable personal visitation of God's Spirit and revelation from Him:

> *I have experienced some blessed teachings of his Holy Spirit ...*
> *I have been more enlightened to see the mystery of godliness,*
> *God manifest in the flesh, and behold more and more of God's*
> *goodness ... I would not have lost this voyage for a thousand*
> *worlds; it has been sweet and profitable to my soul. Lord I want*
> *to know myself and you. Oh let not the hurry of business, which*
> *awaits me on the shore, prevent me hearing the still small voice*
> *of your Holy Spirit.*[5]

The Bible is the objective, normative means of revelation. But although it is normative, it is not exclusive. This remains an ongoing tension within the evangelical church. Does God speak exclusively or only primarily and normatively through Scripture?

Can we expect personal revelations by the Spirit, independent of Scripture, though consistent with it? Luther said no, and argued that in Scripture alone could we find the word of God. Similarly, although Calvin emphasized the necessity of the activity of the Spirit to bring revelation, it was always to the Bible that he directed believers. Luther vehemently, and no doubt rightly, protested against the "Radical Reformers" like Bodenstein, Karlstadt, and Muntzer who, he believed, placed the internal testimony of the Spirit before the external testimony of the Scriptures, thus elevating the personal prophetic illumination.[6]

While we must avoid the introspection of Quakerism with its "inner light," or the subjectivism of German Pietism, or the enthusiasms of the Radical Reformers, and while we want to be rooted and grounded in Scripture, we nevertheless should also say that God still speaks and reveals Himself outside of it. The Bible itself never claims to be the only place God speaks: God speaks through creation (Rom. 1:18f.); conscience (2:14); the *kerygma*[7] (10:14–17); and by the Spirit through dreams, visions, words of knowledge, prophecy, and tongues interpreted (Acts 2:1–21; 1 Cor. 12:8–10). That dynamic, charismatic work of the Spirit in bringing revelation is shown in Scripture as *normative*. Sensitivity to the Spirit's voice is part of the "more" I am calling for—both through Scripture and alongside it, though subject to scriptural norms.

KNOWING WHAT WE HAVE IN GOD

> *... having the eyes of your hearts enlightened that you may know what is the hope to which He has called you, the riches of His glorious inheritance in the saints ...*

Paul will have taught the Ephesians in part, but he wants God to reveal the truths to them. God wants us to know and appreciate who we are and what He has laid up for us through Christ. He wants us to know it for our own joy, peace, assurance, and well-being; He wants us to know that we might stand in the day of trial; He wants us to know that we might give Him the glory He is due. Scripture teaches us, but the Holy Spirit can personally reveal to us the truths contained therein.

The glorious gospel graces presented by Paul in Ephesians 1:3–14 need to be "fully known" by the Ephesians—not merely heard, read, and intellectually understood. Paul prays for the Spirit to reveal these riches to the saints. But he also speaks of "the riches of the glorious inheritance in the saints." It is also possible to read this as "the saints who are His [Christ's] glorious rich inheritance." That we are His inheritance in heaven is a remarkable truth, but a more normal reading would be that God, through Christ, has opened up a great treasure for us. "No eye has seen, no ear has heard, no mind has conceived what God has prepared for those who love Him" (1 Cor. 2:9).

My six-year-old son Joel has a piggy bank. In it are just a few pounds from his allowance. But he excitedly tells everyone, even complete strangers, how much he has. He is not yet at the stage where this is a boast, intended to make others jealous—he is simply delighting in what his dad has given him. My father collects blue and white Chinese porcelain and he often says, "One day all this will be yours, son." (Thanks very much, Dad, but I'd rather you sell it and give me the cash!) God has laid up a great storehouse of riches in heaven. He wants us to walk in the sheer delight and confidence of that glorious inheritance, drawing on some of that trust fund now. I had a friend who used to say, when we met in prayer and when he preached, "Let's plunder the treasure chest of our inheritance!" He knows Christ has opened up heaven to him, and he is not going to waste a thing, or wait until he gets there.

John Bunyan, the famous Nonconformist writer and author, wrote of a revelation he received by the Spirit one day when he was crossing a field. God said to him:

> *"Thy righteousness is in heaven." And me thought withal I*
> *saw with the eye of my soul Jesus Christ at God's right hand.*

I saw, moreover, that it was not my good frame of heart that made my righteousness better, not yet my bad frame that made my righteousness worse; for my righteousness was Jesus Christ Himself, the same yesterday, today and forever. Now did my chains fall from my legs indeed; I was loosed from my afflictions and irons. Oh me thought, Christ, Christ, there was nothing but Christ that was before my eyes! I could look from myself to Him and should reckon that all those graces of God that now were green to me, were yet like those crack groats and four pence halfpennies that rich men carry in their purses, when their gold is in their trunks at home. Oh, I saw my gold was in my trunk at home. In Christ my Lord and saviour. Now Christ was all; all my wisdom, all my righteousness, all my sanctification, all my redemption.[8]

Oh, how different our lives would be, how free from anxiety, depression, jealousy, and discontent, how full of joy and praise, how easy to pray, how quick to praise, if only we could grasp what God has done for us, given us, made us in Christ. But we need the Spirit to take the Word of God and break through those years of lies and sin to help us truly know what He has laid up for us in our heavenly chests.

We are sometimes like the prodigal son (Luke 15:11f.): We may have turned for home, but we have pushed the Father off from hugging us, refused the ring, the sandals, the cloak, and the party. The Spirit wants to come and show us and place around us the embrace of the Father, the signs of dignity, authority, sonship, and delight in us.

KNOWING THE POWER OF GOD

... the immeasurable greatness of His power for us who believe ...

We are not promised just a trickle, but the "immeasurable greatness of His power to us who believe." This power is the promise of Christ, the promise of Pentecost (Acts 1:8). Jesus said we would be "clothed with that power" (Luke 24:49). The Greek word for power is *dunamis*—from which we have derived words like *dynamite*, *dynamo*, and *dynamic*. Christians who are filled with the Holy Spirit will be explosive; they will make a noise and have an impact. Their words, lives, and presence will change things. It is the fullness of that power that Paul wants us to enter into.

Paul declared that the kingdom of God is not a matter of talk but of power (1 Cor. 4:20). Sadly, however, we often seem all talk and no power. Impotent, academic, and anemic, we have placed God in a box; we have domesticated God and rarely want Him to disturb us. But the Scriptures reveal a God who is all power, who breaks our boxes, shatters our bonds, shakes whole rooms, and turns the world upside down and right-side up. This Holy Spirit power was always the mark of the men and women of God in Scripture—power to challenge crooked kings, power to open up seas, power to stop the rain, power to raise the dead, power to overcome one's enemies, power to establish God's kingdom, power to witness to Christ, power to renounce the world, the flesh, and the Devil, power to forgive those who sin against us, power to lay down one's life as a martyr.

John Stott has written, "What we need is not more learning, not more eloquence, not more persuasion, not more organization, but more power from the Holy Spirit."[9] James Stuart Stewart, that great

Scottish preacher of the last century, said, "The new Era of the Spirit has broken in with power. Until we recapture this apostolic perspective and emphasis, our preaching [and our church, lives, witness] will be maimed and crippled."[10]

I have already referred to D. L. Moody's glorious encounter with the Holy Spirit in New York that transformed his ministry. Here is what happened leading up to that. Following one service, two elderly ladies approached him and said, "You are good, but you haven't got it … we have been praying for you … you need power!" Moody, already a well-respected minister, was unimpressed. "I need power?" asked Moody. "Why, I thought I had power!" The ladies poured out their hearts that he might receive the anointing of the Holy Ghost, and soon there grew a great hunger in his soul. "I felt I did not want to live any longer if I had not this power for service." There began a period of six months' pleading with God for more. Then God visited him as he walked down Wall Street in New York; he was never the same again. Although his sermons and doctrine had not changed, his effectiveness in winning thousands to Christ was evidence of this new power. His subsequent ministry saw results of revival proportions in the United States and throughout the British Isles, including all the provinces.[11] There was a particular effectiveness in Cambridge University, where many were won for Christ, filling Ridley Hall with converted ordinands, sending out numerous missionaries, including C. T. Studd, founder of WEC, the largest missionary organization in the world.[12]

One of the major features of so-called renewal theology is a passion to retrace the biblical steps to God's power. Although we must be very careful of the pursuit of power for its own sake or for self-glory, most of us desire more of God's power because we are tired of personal or moral defeat in our lives, tired of ineffective witness, tired of being on the end of Satan's boot rather than vice versa. However, this is not simply a desire that God would "bless me," but that God would "bless others through me." This is not power simply for my benefit, but for others. Without God, I am useless both to myself and to everyone else. But once I have experienced that transforming power of God, that Holy Spirit power that is the source of life (Gen. 1:1) and the presence of love (Eph. 3:16f.), then I may be useful to others, God's power working through me. It was not merely conviction but unction, the power of God, that motivated and energized the radical and reforming saints like St. Francis, Savonarola, Luther, Wesley, Shaftsbury, Wilberforce, Booth, and Teresa.

William Barclay wrote, "The days of the early Church [were] days in which obviously the church seethed and surged with power."[13] Those early Christians had no degrees from the best universities, they had been on no MBA management courses, gone through no psychological Myers-Briggs compatibility profiles, they had no financial investment portfolios—but they had a revelation of God, a revelation of their inheritance in Christ and Holy Spirit power from on high. With this God took 120 people and shook the world.

CHAPTER 4

FURTHER UP AND FURTHER IN

*"Don't stop! Further up and further in," called
Farsight ... Jewel also cried out: "Don't stop.
Further up and further in! Take it in your stride."*

*His voice could only just be heard above the roar
of the water but next moment everyone saw that
he had plunged into the Pool. And helter-skelter
behind him, with splash after splash, all the others
did the same ... They all found they were swimming
straight for the Waterfall itself.*[1]

I suspect that if we could hear that great cloud of witnesses, the
saints who have gone before and who have swum into the depths of
the river of God's Spirit, we would hear them chorus to us, "Don't
stop! Further up and further in!" If we could hear the angels, we
would hear them crying, "Don't stop! Further up and further in!"
And if we could hear the voice of God, we would hear Him bid us

come—"Deep calls to deep in the roar of your waterfalls" (Ps. 42:7
NIV), for that longing many of us have for more of God echoes the
longing that God has for more of us, and His desire to give more of
Himself to us.

Nye Bevan, a Labour cabinet minister in the 1950s and a former
trade union negotiator, walked out of a meeting between the management and the union one day in tears. Asked by the reporters why he
was so obviously upset, he replied, "I am heartbroken by the paucity
of their expectation." For many reasons, many of us have simply no
expectation that God has more of Himself to give us. Others have
simply lost their appetite for the things of God and are content just
to plod on in spiritual mediocrity until they reach heaven. God is
heartbroken.

Those who know me know I am a good eater. The scales prove
the point. I like those pizzerias that offer "all you can eat." I simply
love the idea that you can keep coming back for more, and the only
limit to consumption is your own capacity for pizza. My great friend
Joseph Steinberg[2] holds the record by virtue of having eaten four whole
pizzas—twenty-four slices! Joe has a big girth and a big appetite, but
not just for pizza. This is a man who is hungry for God. I have known
him to get on planes and cross oceans because he has heard a whisper
that God was visiting some place. For years he read eight chapters of
the Bible a day—the whole Bible through twice yearly—because he
was hungry for God. It is no surprise to me that he is now one of the
outstanding evangelists in Britain today. God saw his hunger, God met
him, God filled and now flows out of him.

This Oliver Twist "Please, sir, may I have some more?" attitude
is one God delights in and one we need to incorporate in our own

lives. God has so much more to give us and, whereas it may be bad form to keep going back for more pizza in a restaurant, it is bad form not to come and avail ourselves of all that Christ purchased for us with His blood.

A GLORIOUS INVITATION

One of the most glorious words ever uttered by God is "come." Where else but with God do you find an offer like this: "Come, everyone who thirsts, come to the waters, and he who has no money, come, buy and eat! Come, buy wine and milk without money and without price" (Isa. 55:1)? God did not stop at sending invitations through His prophets. He came in person, and hand-delivered the invitation through Jesus: "Come to Me, all you who are weary and heavy laden, and I will give you rest" (Matt. 11:28); "I am the bread of life; whoever comes will never go hungry" (John 6:35); "If anyone thirsts, let him come to Me and drink" (John 7:37); "Let the little children come to me" (Mark 10:14 NIV); "Come, follow me" (Luke 18:22 NIV); "Come, you who are blessed by My Father, inherit the kingdom prepared for you from the foundation of the world" (Matt. 25:34). The weary, the hungry, the thirsty, the lonely, the lost, all are invited to come—and we can keep coming back. The tragedy is that only some come, and of those, few keep coming further up and further in.

Another glorious invitation is the divine word *ask*. In my family we have a saying, "I wants don't get!" My two sons have a habit of saying, "I want ... a cookie, a DVD on, some juice ..." and we reply, "I wants don't get!" They usually then say, "Please may I have ..." and, smiling at our so-polite young chaps, we give in to their requests. God, however, may not be so bothered about Ps and Qs. Indeed, Jesus tells us to come to Him like little children. God never uses the phrase, "I wants don't get." On the contrary, a respectful "Dear God, I want ..." is quite likely to raise a smile from Him and open His hand. In John 17:24, Jesus Himself sets the example: "Father, I want that they also ..." as well as exhorting us to ask of Him (16:24).

When I was about twelve, my teachers gave me a day off school to visit the council chambers where my mother worked. We were driven there in a Rolls-Royce by a wealthy politician friend of the family. After a long, boring debate about the lines of drains or road tarmac (I forget), we went for lunch. The owner of the Rolls asked me if I would like a Coke. To this day I do not know where this came from, but suddenly I replied, "No, thank you, but I'd quite like one of your cigars!"

My mother was furious, not only because I wanted to smoke underage, but mainly because I had embarrassed her by asking her friend for an expensive cigar when I was offered a Coke. Spluttering on her coffee, she swiftly rebuked me. But the man smiled, apparently appreciating my cheeky boldness. Chuckling, he took out a leather case and handed me a very expensive cigar. Before Mum could slap me, I left the room, rustled up a match, and lit this ten-inch cigar. It was foul—put me off cigars for life! But I learned an important principle: If you ask, you just might get—but make sure it is something you want! Now the Lord will not give us anything illegal or harmful, but He delights to offer, and He responds to bold presumption. It shows that we take Him seriously.

In the context of teaching His disciples about prayer (Luke 11:5f.), Jesus tells the parable of a man who had an unexpected visitor at midnight. Out of food, and needing to show hospitality to his guest, he goes to a neighboring friend, wakes him up, and asks for some bread. Describing the reluctance on the part of the sleepy (and now grumpy) neighbor to stir himself out of bed, Jesus says that although the neighbor will not get up and give him the bread simply because they are neighbors, he will get up and give the bread because of the friend's *anaideian*—his persistence or impudence. Jesus continues:

> *And I tell you, ask, and it will be given to you; seek, and you will find; knock, and it will be opened to you. For everyone who asks receives, and the one who seeks finds, and to the one who knocks it will be opened. What father among you, if his son asks for a fish, will instead of a fish give him a serpent; or if he asks for an egg, will give him a scorpion? If you then, who are evil, know how to give good gifts to your children, how much more will the heavenly Father give the Holy Spirit to those who ask him! (Luke 11:9–13 ESV)*

What we have here is an encouragement to be expectant and persistent in prayer. God, a loving and generous Father, promises that He will respond by giving us the good gift of "more of the Holy Spirit." He promises us more of the presence, power, glory, gifting, intimacy, and character-transforming work of God in our lives. James says, "You do not have, because you do not ask God" (4:2

NIV). So why don't more believers ask for more of God? Perhaps they don't know they should ask, or that there is anything else to ask for. Others may be content with what they have, or don't think they will be heard. And maybe some don't ask because they don't think they are worthy to ask for anything.

But the promise is there, in black and white on the printed page, and in crimson-red blood on the cross. God is a promise-maker and a promise-keeper, but are we promise-seekers and promise-takers? When was the last time you asked God for "more of the Holy Spirit"? Jesus said, "He gives the Spirit without measure" (John 3:34).

In the Old Testament, God appears to Solomon at night (2 Chron. 1:7) and asks him to ask: "Ask. What shall I give you?" Solomon asks for wisdom and knowledge, and because he does not ask for riches or power over his enemies, God is pleased to grant him this, and also that which he does not ask for (v. 12). With God we get not only more than we deserve, but more than we expect. If God were to appear to you tonight, what would you ask Him for?

HANDBRAKES ON THE HOLY SPIRIT

Despite the invitation from God in His Word and His constant wooing by the Spirit, despite the illustrations throughout Scripture and church history of God responding to those who press in hard after Him, there still seems to be a reluctance on the part of many Christians. What exigencies act against our pursuit of more of God?

1. An unexpectant heart

Many Christians seem blind to the promises and prayers in Scripture that indicate an ever-increasing deepening in our experience of God, knowledge of God, and power from God. Many have not, because they ask not, because they expect not, because they know not. Often our churchmanship conditions us and sets parameters and limits on what is appropriate and what we may legitimately expect from God. We are so often like the Ephesians (Acts 19:1f.), who, when Paul asks them if they received the Holy Spirit when they believed, reply somewhat bemusedly, "No, we have not even heard that there is a Holy Spirit." Many have lived their Christian lives in such a small box that they do not know what God is giving and doing elsewhere, and are too afraid to even look, lest they be led astray. We are like Tolkien's typical hobbit, wrapped up in our own little Shire: We do not know what is beyond the borders—danger, but also adventure and treasure—and we do not want to know.

At the risk of oversimplification and parody,[3] let me set out what strikes me about the different streams of churchmanship. The contemplative has faith, expectancy, and an experience of meeting God in the solitary desert place of withdrawal unto God. Prayer, silence, and meditation are the means for practicing the presence of God. The evangelical has faith, expectancy, and experience to believe that God will meet one at conversion to Christ, as one studies Scripture or sits under the sound teaching, and as one engages in evangelistic "gospel work." The sacramentalist has faith, expectancy, and experience that God will meet one through the initiation of baptism and confirmation, and primarily through the priestly administration of the Eucharist and confessional. The theological liberal has faith, expectancy, and experience to believe that one encounters God abroad in the world, often through various sociopolitical moves that seek to minister God's loving kindness and justice to the poor and oppressed. The Pentecostal has faith, expectancy, and experience to believe that God will meet us in power, with gifts following, by the Holy Spirit through prayer and the laying on of hands. The holiness tradition has faith, expectancy, and experience to believe that God may be known through the pursuit of a virtuous, holy life, lived in radical distinction and separation from the world.

Through spiritual pride these variant streams have usually been isolated from each other, with little overlap or mutual sharing between traditions. "We drink from our own wells." This of course limits our experience and expectancy of the activity of God's Spirit, confining it to restricted and artificial parameters set up by our spiritual fathers and their particular articulation and succession of the biblical or ecclesiastical traditions. Interestingly, Richard Foster believes that we live in a day when the Spirit of God is seeking to take all that is divinely authentic in each tradition and to join these various streams into one mighty river of blessing: "It is a deep river of divine intimacy, a powerful river of holy living, a dancing river of jubilation in the Spirit, and a broad river of unconditional love for all peoples."[4]

2. An unyielded life

The Spirit comes to make Jesus Lord in our lives (1 Cor. 12:3). The Spirit transforms us into the likeness of Christ (2 Cor. 3:18f.), removing the sinful human nature (Gal. 5:16–21), and conforms us to the sweet divine character (vv. 22f.). The Spirit comes to lead, direct, and govern us (vv. 18, 22), and to empower us for service and witness to Christ (Acts 1:8). This Spirit of God is sovereign—not merely for our benefit, but to use us for His. This Holy Spirit, this divine dynamite, is dangerous. He blows where He wills, He goes where He wills, He will take us where He wills, He will break us as He wills, He will make us as He wills, He will use us as He wills (John 3:8).

But some of us do not want that. We want to be in control, we want to be lord, we want to indulge the flesh, we do not want to witness and work for Christ, we want God on our terms and our conditions. We do not want Him interfering, going where He is not welcome. We want Him to serve us, not us to serve Him. We want to ask Him for things, not Him to ask us. We want a certain autonomy, a day off, some off-limits areas.

This unyielded life will never know and grow in God. The church is full of saved but stunted spiritual pygmies. The person who would have more of God must give more to God. The person who would hear God more must listen more to God. The person who would be filled with the Spirit must relinquish all rights. The Spirit must have free rein through our whole lives, without any compartmentalizing or qualifying what He may do or where He may go. Do you desire more of God? Then yield to Him. Surrender is the only way to live life in the Spirit. Samuel Chadwick saw this key to unlocking heaven's blessing: "Things not surrendered, indulgences retained against light, possessions held or selfish ends—these must all be surrendered to the supreme authority of

Christ. For until he is exalted, crowned, glorified, there can be no Pentecost."[5]

Billy Graham, already established in his ministry, felt frustrated and as if he was living at second best.[6] At a conference he woke up another guest speaker in the middle of the night to talk over his difficulties. This speaker was Edwin Orr, a famous historian of revival. As Graham expressed his hunger for "deeper blessing," Orr told him it came by way of surrender. Orr probed Graham: "Have you surrendered your will, emotions, intellect?"

Graham went out alone that night. There was one issue that he knew was holding him back—an issue that needed to be "put to death." After deep wrestlings he surrendered this issue to the Lord. He returned saying that he had been filled afresh with the Spirit of God and had received a vision for his ministry. A revival shortly followed him to Los Angeles, and his newfound power and authority astounded all.

3. An unconfessed sin

The Holy Spirit is called the Holy Spirit precisely because He is holy. He cannot abide sin or abide with sin. The Spirit of God departed from Saul following his disobedience, rebellion, and pride (1 Sam. 16:14). David in his adultery and treachery with Bathsheba knew the fear of God's absence. Repenting, he begged, "Take not Thy Holy Spirit from me" (Ps. 51:11). The promise of Peter at Pentecost was, "Repent and be baptized for the forgiveness of sins, and you will receive the Holy Spirit" (Acts 2:38).

If we desire more of God's Spirit in our lives, revealing Christ, transforming our characters, empowering our service, we must repent and renounce anything that is offensive to Him. As young Christians, we may renounce the more obvious sins of immorality, idolatry, and involvement with occult practices. But increasingly, as we seek more, we will find the Spirit putting His finger on attitudes, passions, conversations, and motivations. The Spirit shines the spotlight on our sins of commission (what we do) and our sins of omission (what we fail to do). Only as we repent and surrender these areas do we find the Spirit taking over that cleansed part of us, filling it with His presence, power, and active control.

The South African David Du Plessis, once welcomed by the pope as "Mr. Pentecost,"[7] was remarkably used by God to cross-fertilize the Pentecostal blessing with the mainline denominations. As a young boy he had read in Scripture and heard testimonies that there was more power from on high by the Holy Spirit, and he desired this passionately. Asking his teacher for the day off school, he told his parents he was going to spend the day in the barn seeking God for what he termed "the baptism in the Spirit." All day he sought God in prayer, fasting, and tears, but nothing came. Utterly frustrated, he was about to give up when a friend of his came to the barn and was led by the Spirit to say, "If you confess that sin, you will get it." Instantly he knew what God was highlighting, a lie that he had intentionally told his parents some years before. He went to them to confess this sin, and almost immediately was powerfully drenched with God's Holy Spirit, speaking in tongues. This young man went on to become the general secretary of the World Pentecostal Conferences, a much-respected ecumenist, welcomed at Vatican II, and used by God to bring the historic denominations into a greater appreciation and experience of the Holy Spirit. But it all began with a hunger for more and a confession of sin.

4. An undiscerned enemy

Who has most to gain from you gaining least from God? We have already noted Tozer's comment that "Satan has opposed the doctrine of the Spirit-filled life about as bitterly as any other doctrine there is,"[8] and it does not take a rocket scientist to deduce why. The believer who has laid hold of all that God has laid up for him or her in Christ is the one who walks in freedom from the grips of the evil one. If Satan cannot keep us from coming to Christ, he will keep us from coming closer to Christ. If he cannot hinder our salvation, he will seek to hinder our sanctification. He desires to have a hold on our lives and will not relinquish those footholds of sin and bondage without a fight.

The thing Satan most dreads, having seen us renounce him and receive Christ, is that we in turn will be used by God to establish the kingdom in the lives of others. The Spirit-filled Christian who has tasted of the powers of the kingdom to come (Heb. 6:4f.), who is fully consecrated to the Savior, loving His presence, listening to His voice, learning His Word, available to be used by God, is an awesome weapon. "Those who know their God shall be strong and shall do exploits" (Dan. 11:32). Not only is the Spirit-filled believer, anointed by God's power and equipped with God's gifts, able to be more powerfully used by God in plundering the domain of the Enemy, but the Spirit-filled Christian also has a greater discernment of the spiritual battle.

Such a person is also more able to recognize, resist, and rout the works of the Enemy. The anointing of the Holy Spirit and His increased activity in one's life exposes the activity and the territory where the Enemy has influence. It is the experience of many that as soon as they enter into the fullness of the Spirit, receiving a fresh anointing, empowering, and revelation from God, they join a battle as the Enemy seeks to take back the kingdom ground gained in and potentially through that individual. I did not know I needed deliverance from afflicting demons until I received a greater filling of the Spirit. But the more I made myself available to the Holy Spirit, the more He shone the spotlight on the dark areas, those strongholds of the Enemy that needed to be set free by the Word of God and cleansed by the blood of Christ. The anointing of the Holy Spirit reveals demonic shadows that are dispatched through repentance, renunciation, and the authoritative Word of God applied by faith. Sometimes simply a sincere opening up of our lives to the Holy Spirit will uproot demonic footholds.

David MacInnes, whose leadership in the early charismatic renewal led him into a powerful deliverance ministry, says that when the Spirit moves, it will immediately provoke a conflict with the demonic power whose territory is being challenged. Cardinal Suenens says that renewal of the Holy Spirit:

> *sensitises Christians to the reality of the world of darkness,*
> *the world which the Spirit rejects. It is giving them a new*
> *awareness of the reality of the Adversary (Jn 16:8). The Holy*
> *Spirit awakens the malevolence of Evil … The Holy Spirit gives*
> *those who open themselves to him a sharper perception that*
> *enables them to see, to denounce and to fight against everything*
> *in the world that is a negation of God … The Holy Spirit*
> *awakens us to the necessity of spiritual combat …*[9]

After Christ's baptism in water and filling with the Holy Spirit (Luke 4:1), the Spirit immediately leads Him into the wilderness. Instantly there is a cosmic confrontation with the Devil, who has been active, but scripturally incognito, for hundreds of years. The anointing of the Holy Spirit causes him to surface and challenge Jesus' identity and authority as the divine Son. The ultimate purpose of this power encounter is to deflect Christ from His intended mission. Being Spirit filled did not end the battle, it caused Jesus to enter it. Returning from this sifting time, Jesus visits the synagogue, where immediately a demonic spirit manifests before the Spirit-anointed Jesus, and is quickly dispatched by His authoritative word (v. 33).

In Ephesians, Paul repeatedly reminds us of our identity and our inheritance in Christ, and then prays for a greater anointing of the Holy Spirit. He commands the Ephesians not to grieve the Holy Spirit, but to seek more of the Spirit's fullness, that they might live a holy life. Paul concludes with a challenge to be strengthened by God's mighty power (His Holy Spirit), that we might engage in spiritual battle with the demonic forces (Eph. 5:11f.), who are defeated by believers standing in the finished work of Christ and taking the sword of the Spirit and praying in the Spirit (6:17). St. Augustine, drawing on the imagery of the psalmist, said it is the Holy Spirit who trains our hands for battle and our fingers for war.[10]

Sadly, to most Christians, even many evangelicals, the Devil is almost a myth. Not taken seriously, not challenged vigorously, he is able to act surreptitiously. But I guarantee that if you seek to live more in the life and power of the Spirit, you will sooner rather than later confront the Devil. However, only the Spirit-filled Christian can withstand the onslaught of the enemy. As C. T. Studd said,

> *When in hand-to-hand conflict with the world and the devil,*
> *neat little biblical confectionary is like shooting lions with*
> *a pea-shooter; one needs a man who will let himself go and*
> *deliver blows right and left as hard as he can hit, trusting in*
> *the Holy Ghost ... Nothing but forked lightning Christians*
> *will count!* [11]

5. An unclaimed inheritance

In Numbers 32 we read of the tribes of Gad and Reuben arriving at the Jordan River on the edge of the Promised Land. But the land of Jazer and Gilead, whose peoples had been defeated, was land that was good for livestock and these two tribes had a great number of animals. The tribal leaders requested of Moses that they be allowed to stay there, rather than cross the Jordan, and to claim this land as their inheritance (vv. 1–5). Moses is furious. This is a threat to the unity of Israel and a negation of their necessary commitment to assist their fellow Israelites in the fighting to claim the land (vv. 6–15). He sees in them the same spirit of their forefathers who refused to enter the Promised Land and died wandering through the desert.

The Gadite and Reubenite leaders suggest a compromise (vv. 16–19): that they be allowed to have this land, to build sheepfolds and pens for the animals and homes for their families, on the condition that they accompany Israel into the Promised Land and fight with them until the land is won and all have their inheritance. Only then will they return to their land, families, and livestock. To this Moses agrees, and he formulates a binding covenant with these two tribes (vv. 25–32).

But this land that was good and sweet and favorable for their cattle and won from their enemy—was this what God had in mind for them? Yes, they are out of Egypt; yes, they are at rest in the land; yes, they prosper under God's provision. But this is not the place of promise. They settle on the wrong side, on the east of the Jordan. They never enter their promised inheritance in the land of Canaan, west of the Jordan.[12] They have settled for too little, they have failed to avail themselves of the promise, they are living beneath their inheritance and their birthright. They were not brought out of Egypt to stay east of the Jordan and to settle for the first bit of good land they see.

Many Christians have failed to cross the Jordan into the Promised Land. They have arrived at the Jordan, but establish their lives to the east rather than the west of it. They know deliverance from Egypt, defeat of their enemies, and live in a place of provision, but they do not inhabit the place of full promise. Later we will see how many Christians live experientially somewhere between Romans 5 and Romans 8: They know justification by faith and reconciliation with God, but they have yet to cross the Jordan into that intimate life in the Spirit as sons of God.

It is remarkable how many millions have won the lottery but failed to claim their winnings. Recently a television advertisement in the UK stated that billions of pounds of social security benefits payments belong to people who have not filled out the forms to receive their due. Similarly we have blessings in Christ that we have not taken because we have not known about then. The Spirit, the promised gift of God (Luke 24:49; Acts 1:4; Gal. 3:14), mediates our inheritance in Christ to us. He takes us across the Jordan, from east to west, into the Land of Promise. Sadly many, like those Gadites and Reubenites, have even assisted others to enter the land, but have never enjoyed living in it themselves.

Judges 2:6 says, "The people went and took possession of the land, each to his inheritance." I read of a woman in Hull in 1999 who won several million pounds in the lottery but refused to claim it. The press somehow hunted her down and finally, through the encouragement of family and friends, convinced her to claim what was hers. Just ten minutes before the cutoff moment, she redeemed her ticket and winnings. Oh, how sad it is that many go for so long in their Christian life without appropriating all that Christ died to bring us, even before we join Him in the age to come.

6. Unwanted gifts

One of the main unclaimed areas in church life that the Holy Spirit renewal movement has shown us is that of the spiritual gifts (*charismata* in Greek; see 1 Cor. 12:4—word of wisdom, word of knowledge, faith, healing, miracles, prophecy, discernment of spirits, tongues, interpretation of tongues). Despite the plethora of books, both popular and academic, that have been published on the matter in the past thirty years, the convincing arguments for these gifts as normative for the church today and the considerable documentation evidencing the gifts throughout church history, the actual manifestation of them in the everyday life of the church remains disappointing.[13] It seems that "charismatic" these days, far from referring to a church exercising the nine gifts of the Spirit listed in 1 Corinthians 12, is sometimes more likely to imply lively and prolonged music from a plugged-in band with hands waved in the air. That is not what Paul would term charismatic. For him these charisms, supernatural manifestations of the Holy Spirit, were to be exercised in the regular daily life of the church and the weekly corporate worship. Church was to be a place where healings, miracles, deliverances, prophecies, and revelations were to occur. Paul tells us that we are not to be ignorant of the gifts (1 Cor. 12:1), and we are not to be indifferent to the gifts (v. 31; 14:1). Rather we are eagerly to desire them—to pursue them and to practice them, not for self-indulgence, but for the mutual building up of the church (12:7; 14:4).

Judson Cornwall tells the story of a dream he had when he was the pastor of a small church in the United States that experienced a wonderful move of the Spirit and a newfound release of spiritual gifts.[14] In this dream he saw his congregation in a large department store. Over the sound system the words kept coming loud and clear, "Take whatever you want—it's free. Take whatever you want—it's free." He noticed that all around on tables and shelves were many items, and his church members were stuffing their pockets with them. But he also noted that they were all mere trinkets, and yet he saw that higher up on the shelves were very expensive goods. He began calling out to his people, "Look higher! Look higher!" but they could not hear him. He awoke from the dream weeping at what he felt was a tragic opportunity lost. He shared the dream with his church and said that he felt God was encouraging them not to be sidetracked by lesser things, but to go deeper with God. They could not understand him, he may not have made himself plain, but eventually he resigned, sensing that they had closed the door to the "more" God would give them.

Twenty years later he was invited back to the dedication of a new part of the church building. At the dinner afterward one woman remarked, "Oh, Pastor, isn't it wonderful? We still have all those gifts which God gave us in that renewal when you were here twenty years ago."[15] Hardly able to contain himself, Judson excused himself from the party, returned to his hotel, and fell on his bed weeping. Yes, they still had the same old gifts, the same old ministries. In fact everything and everyone was just the same.

They did not appear to have grown or received anything new from God in twenty years. Have you?

7. Unbelief because of unworthiness

David MacInnes, with forty years of experience ministering in renewal, believes this to be the greatest obstacle to personal renewal in the Spirit. Not unbelief in the existence of such gifts or such encounters with God, but unbelief that God would ever give such gifts or make Himself known to us. It is possible that we have not sought God with all our heart (Jer. 29:13; Matt. 7:7). It is possible we have sought Him with a mercenary motive (John 6:26), desiring the gifts without the Giver. Sometimes we have sought and not found and have concluded that we can never receive: Rather than press through, we pass it up. But more commonly, I believe, we listen to the Devil, who is always fostering the lie that there is nothing more, certainly not for us. This creature of condemnation would rob us of our new-birth rights.

Paul says, however, "He who did not spare His own Son, but gave Himself up for us, will He not freely give us all things?" (Rom. 8:32). If you feel that you are not worthy to receive "more," then you are right.

You are not. But gifts are not based on the merit of the recipient, but on the generosity of the giver. God's heart is one of love for you. And He has more to give you. He has written a love letter in His own blood to show you the extent of His love. I play a game with my boys: I ask them, "How much do you love me?" and they reply, "To the moon and back; to the sun and back; twice round the world and back." God says, "I love you from heaven to earth and back; to hell and back." You are the apple of His eye, accepted in the Beloved, His pearl of great price, someone worth dying for, someone He wants to spend forever with. If you do not feel this, you are exactly the one who needs to pray Paul's prayer for yourself from Ephesians 3:14–19.

Now I'd like us to study some of our biblical ancestors who let nothing, no obstacles, stand in the way of their receiving all and more of what God wants to offer.

A GRITTY DETERMINATION

Throughout history God's men and women have been marked by the tenacity and desire for more of God in and through their lives. This holy discontent and holy desire has marked all the greats of the church: "The kingdom of God advances forcefully and forceful men lay hold of it" (Matt. 11:12).

Jacob

Scripture and tradition consistently tell us that those who gained most of God and were used most by God went most for God. Thus we meet Jacob, a rather sly, deceitful twister of a character with almost no redeeming qualities. But there is one thing that characterizes him, both negatively and positively, and which God takes and uses to be a blessing to the nations: This man will not settle for second best. Jacob was marked by a fiery discontent and a passion for more. Even in his mother's womb, with his twin Esau, he wrestled rather than nestled (Gen. 25:22).

Although Jacob is the second to leave the womb, he holds on to his sibling's heel: "Don't you think you're getting ahead of me!"[16] The father's blessing and the birthright of being the family head go to the elder twin, Esau, but Jacob will not settle for second best. He feels destiny surging in his veins—and when his brother returns from the field exhausted and hungry, he presumptuously offers a meal in exchange for the birthright. (Esau, contemptibly, is easily bought off [Gen. 25:29f.].) When their father, Isaac, is an old man and ready to bow out, he prepares to give his blessing, but first he desires a meal from his elder son, Esau. But this blessing, this birthright, unbeknown to Isaac, has already been bought by Jacob. And while Esau is off in the fields hunting a last meal for Isaac, Jacob prepares a meal, pretends to be Esau, and receives the irreversible anointing, the blessing of his father (Gen. 27).

This striving for more, this refusal of mediocrity, is also shown in the way Jacob wins the desire of his heart, Rachel, and in his business dealings with his father-in-law, as he amasses a flock worth a fortune (Gen. 29—31). He has not accepted his lot, he has not accepted the status given to him at his birth, the preeminence of his brother, or the contrivance of his father-in-law. This man is marked by destiny and tenacity. In a mysterious and marvelous passage (Gen. 32:22–32), we see Jacob laying hold of his destiny. One night he meets God, who visits him in theophanic form as a man.

Through the night Jacob wrestles with God, yet as the sun rises, he is still struggling and still standing. The Lord reminds him that kneeling before God is the appropriate place for man, and merely touches him on the thigh, putting out his joint and causing him to fall to his knees. Yet Jacob is still not letting go, and through gritted teeth he hangs on. The Lord says, "Now will you let Me go?" But Jacob replies with a "not now, not ever": "I will not let You go unless You bless me." *Good*, thinks God. And He blesses Jacob—not because He has to, but because He wants to. Here at last is one worthy to be the father of the nation of God. "No longer will you be called Jacob, the grasper, but Israel, he who strives with God, for you have striven with God and man and prevailed" (Gen. 32:22f.). Jacob prevailed because he had determination. His discontent with his position and his determination were not rebellion. His passion, his motivation, had always been for a blessing. He would not let go until he got what he knew only God could give. He received this blessing, and through it became a blessing to the world.

In the Song of Solomon, four times we see the glorious refrain of the bride, "Him whom my heart loves" (3:1–4). The beloved is momentarily separated from her lover and goes out in search of him. When she finds him, she tells us, "I held him and would not let him go till I had brought him to my mother's house" (3:4). Oh, to have sought and caught and brought the Lord to one's chamber!

Jabez

Amid a list of undistinguished names, people who did nothing to write home about, we meet a man named Jabez (1 Chron. 4:9). The

Bible says simply, "He was more honorable than his brothers." We do not know whether they were "dishonorable," but it seems that the mark of his "honor" was his "hunger" for more from God. His name, Jabez, sounds like the Hebrew for "born in pain," but he refused to have this as a perpetuating prophecy over his life. He was a man who lived for the future, rather than looking to the past. And this man called upon God, saying, "Oh that You would bless me and enlarge my border, and that Your hand might be with me, and that You would keep me from harm so that it might not bring me pain."[17] And God granted what he asked. This man is marked by discontent. Like Jacob he wants God's blessing. It is that which distinguishes him from the other names, that which causes him to open God's heart and hand.

If only some of those other "wonder-less names" had prayed like Jabez. I confess I often get bored reading through those long lists of names in Chronicles—names of people who lived such undistinguished lives, who made no impression either on the chronicler or on their nation's history. I think God is unimpressed as well. I do not want to be another name in a list with nothing to add to it. I want a testimony, I want to be an illustration, I want my life to be a story to the glory of God's grace. Curiosity killed the cat, and mediocrity kills the church. God is looking for a church full of Jabezes who refuse the status quo and who press on until they have gained from God His blessing for them and through them. A. W. Tozer rightly said, "The Church of this moment needs men, the right kind of men, bold men. The talk is that we need revival, that we need a new baptism of the Spirit—and God knows that we must have both; but God will not revive mice. He will not fill rabbits with the Holy Ghost."[18]

Joshua

In Exodus 33:7–11 we meet Joshua in "A Tale of Two Tents." Moses would pitch a tent outside the camp, and "all who sought the Lord would go to this tent of meeting." This was not the tabernacle for the ark of the covenant, the tent of the presence, the place of sacrifice, offering, and forgiveness—that was in the center of the camp (Num. 2:17)—but a second, separate tent, a tent for lovers' trysting.[19] I grew up on the edge of the countryside, and as a young teenager I would build a den out of hay bales at harvest time, hoping to bring a girlfriend there for romantic encounters. (Sadly for my teenage self, my dream was never realized.) But here was a tent where God came and met intimately with His people. Anyone who sought the Lord could go there and inquire of Him, hear from Him, meet Him, and find relief for their boredoms, resolution for their problems. Unlike the Masai people's god, Engai, who is a terribly remote god living far away at the farthest point in the sky,[20] the God of the Bible is a God who makes Himself known, accessible, personal, and intimate. He is always Immanuel, God with us. In this tent God would come down and speak with Moses face-to-face (Ex. 33:11), as with a friend.

Despite the wonderful invitation of the tent, however, there appears to have been a real reluctance on the part of the people to respond to it. Whenever the pillar of cloud indicating the Lord's presence descended on the tent, the people would keep their distance, staying standing within the camp at the entrance to their tents (Ex. 33:10). Yes, they would worship, but from a distance. Why did they not run to the tent? Why did the shout not go out throughout the camp, "The Lord has come!"? Why did everyone not rush to the tent of trysting? Perhaps they were content in the knowledge that their sins were forgiven by their offering of sacrifices at the tabernacle. They did not need any intimacy—just the security of sins forgiven. Perhaps they were content knowing that they had the Ten Commandments and did not need anything else. Perhaps they feared that they might not be welcome. After all, they were not all Joshua or Moses, and God might even turn sour on them—or worse. Perhaps they thought the effort was not worth it, for by the time they got there, God might have left. Perhaps they were waiting for someone else to make the first move, but no one did and they were not prepared to go out on a limb. The presence of the Lord evoked worship, and rightly so, but it should also have evoked a stampede. When I first understood this, I broke down and wept—I was literally convulsed with sobs. Here were God's people, spectators when they could be participators, standing on the sidelines cheering when they could be on the field playing. And I sensed I was feeling something of God's sadness. He is a God who comes to us, but few bother coming to Him.

But the story of the trysting tent does not end there (Ex. 33:11). Someone would not miss out. When Moses returned to the camp, his assistant Joshua, a young man, would not depart from the tent. Why should he? Why would he? God was there! Moses said, "I'm off back to the camp. Are you coming?" And Joshua replied, "I'll be down later, I've unfinished business here." The Israelites were too content to leave their tents. Joshua was not content to leave God's tent. Joshua wanted more of God. He wanted to linger in His presence. What could be more pressing, what could be more precious than this?

Wild horses could not drag him away. "No, Moses, you go—but I'm for staying," he said. The Hebrew tenses in verse 11 show that his abiding at the tent was not a one-off event, but a continuous thing. Whenever[21] Moses returned to the camp, Joshua would always remain. I am sure his family, friends, and peers questioned him. None seem to have joined him. But Joshua put first things first. Time with God was paramount. Everything else could wait. Like Jesus (John 4:32), Joshua had food to eat of which the others knew nothing. But in those times, God was inculcating something in Joshua. As Joshua abided in His presence, God was speaking, showing him things, honing his character, preparing him to lead the people of Israel into the Promised Land. It was those times in the trysting tent that trained and tempered Joshua to be the leader he later became.

Paul

Today the average Christian is pursuing the wrong thing. His heart is in the wrong place. His appetites are after the wrong affections. He is spiritually contented and materially discontented. Happy with where he is with God, unhappy with where he is with his investments, pension fund, possessions. Paul was the opposite. He had learned to be materially content, happy with whatever he had (Phil. 4:11); yet he remained spiritually discontent, hungry to gain more firsthand knowledge of Christ (Phil. 3:10). Kierkegaard said, "Longing is the umbilical cord of the higher life."

Paul refused to settle for too little; he was hungry for more, always seeking to go further up and further in. We have already seen that this was a prayer he prayed repeatedly for the Ephesians and for the Colossians, in the subjunctive mood, that God might give them by the Spirit a greater revelation of Himself and a greater power of the Spirit. In his letter to the Philippians, imprisoned and in chains, Paul is not bitter. In fact the letter resounds with life and the theme of "rejoicing." In chapter 3, Paul is in a reflective mood. Everything that he once had going for him, in terms of his impressive practice of and status within Judaism, he now considers *detritus*, dung, compared to gaining Christ and being made righteous by faith in Christ. This Jesus is worth losing everything for. Nothing can compare with knowing Christ, the resurrection power of the Holy Spirit, the union with Christ by faith and baptism. Hawthorne says that this "knowledge of Christ" that Paul pursues "is not primarily intellectual but experiential … the knowledge of Christ is personal and intimate, as the expression 'my Lord' shows, certainly more than an intellectual apprehension of truth about Christ. Rather, it is a personal appropriation of and communion with Christ himself."[22]

For Paul, however, it does not stop there. He wants more. This glorious salvation and union with Christ simply fuels a desire for more. Paul does not want to sweat it out by waiting until he gets to heaven to appropriate and appreciate what this union with Christ means. He wants now, today, in his chains, in prison, to enter more fully into the mystery of knowing Christ, as the King James translation says, "that I may apprehend that for which also I am apprehended of Christ Jesus" (Phil. 3:12 KJV). He says twice that he has not yet made his own what is his own (vv. 12–13), and he says twice that he is pressing on to make this objective reality his own personal experience.

But wait a minute, Paul—just hang on a second. You are Paul the apostle. You know the Lord better than any of us. You have had personal revelations of God, open visions, visitations to the third heaven; you have been used by God to found the church to the Gentiles. You have seen the dead raised, the lame walk, the demonized delivered. Paul, you have so much: What's all this about "more"? Take it easy, indulge yourself. You are nearing the end of your life—why all this straining and striving? Relax! But Paul replies, "Oh, but there is more, and I won't wait. I am heartbroken by the paucity of your expectation!"

George Whitefield

George Whitefield was discontent with the content of his religion. He looked for a personal and powerful life-transforming experience of Christ.[23] Regularly after supper he would walk in Christ Church meadows just across the way from his Pembroke College. There, under a tree, he would kneel or lie prostrate, desperately seeking God. Renouncing any and all affections that might stand in the way of him and God, even his friendship and membership of the Holy Club, Whitefield hounded the God who would give him no rest. Each morning in the bitter cold he would wake early and seek the face of the Father, fasting and fighting the Devil. He became so emaciated that he was confined to bed, and the physician was summoned. He resolved "to die or to conquer." Ill in bed for seven weeks, he sought and fought for God, repenting of sin, reaching out for the Savior. Although he was weak, he spent two hours daily praying over his Greek New Testament. He would have either a breakthrough or a breakdown, but what he would not have was the mediocrity of his current spiritual state. He was in pursuit, he would not let go until God blessed him—and then God came.[24] One day, somewhere in

Oxford, perhaps during one of his secluded walks in the meadows, it happened:

> *God was pleased to remove the heavy load, to enable me to lay hold of His dear Son by a living faith and by giving me the Spirit of adoption, to seal me even to the day of everlasting redemption. O! with what joy—joy unspeakable—even joy that was full of and big with glory, was my soul filled, when the weight of sin went off, and an abiding sense of the pardoning love of God and a full assurance of faith, broke in upon my disconsolate soul! Surely it was the day of mine espousals [marriage]—a day to be had in everlasting remembrance! At first my joys were like a spring tide, and overflowed the banks!* [25]

This man was transformed, and so saturated by God's power that his preaching sparked a revival in Britain and the Americas. Let us not miss again the features of his experience that reflect those of the biblical, mystical, Pentecostal, charismatic experience tradition when speaking in terms of the fullness of the Spirit: freedom, sonship, assurance of salvation, joy, glory, fullness, deliverance, pardon, love, intimacy, saturation point.

My story

I certainly do not count myself among our biblical ancestors and the great forefathers of our faith, but I thought I might here share my story of how I came to desire more and more of the Spirit.

I was born into a family with a long and strong history of lay leadership in the Nonconformist tradition. On my mother's side were several generations of Exclusive Brethren and on my father's side several generations of Baptists, with Dad a Strict Baptist.

My earliest memories are of church. I am told I went twice every Sunday from the age of two weeks until my midteens. During those childhood days, church was a duty rather than a delight, an "ought" rather than a "want."

At the age of eleven I was immersed in the baptistery at the front of Saltash Baptist Church on public profession of my faith. But like many others, I began to drift from the church, and, by the time I was sixteen, had stopped attending at all. As I approached twenty, a number of incidents precipitated a spiritual crisis in my life, and one night I found myself in the back of a church. The singing and the service so impacted me that I sat, shivering and shaken.

The following Sunday when my mates asked me whether I would be going to the pub with them, I replied, "No, I'm going to church." They thought I was joking, but I had found a better song to sing. This time I sat in the middle and again, during an extended time of singing, those in the church ascended to the heavenlies in tongues. I fought back the tears. God was truly in this place, and rain was falling on the desert of my life. The vicar spoke about the cross, all the while seeming to stare at me. His words pierced my soul and laid me bare.

At the end of the service he invited everyone in the congregation to come forward for prayer, for any reason. My chest was thumping, my legs almost buckling, and my brow sweating. I rushed to the front, and knelt at the altar rail weeping. A dear old chap came to pray for me and tried to glean my name and what was going on, but

I was lost—or being found. Through the snot and tears I ran like the prodigal son back into the arms of the Father as He embraced me. I was home at last.

I loved it. It was like coming awake after a long night of dark dreams. It felt like coming into the sunlight having been in the shadows. I had believed in God, but now I came to know Him. I had an insatiable appetite for Scripture and attended every Bible study I could. I bought a series of commentaries and a fat Bible and hungrily worked my way through it, sometimes spending hours a day in study and prayer.

At one service there was an invitation to come forward to receive a greater release of God's Spirit, and I went for prayer. For the first time I had the laying on of hands, and as those around me prayed, it felt like electricity flowing through my arms, like pins and needles, only not painful. I felt I was being bathed in God. After they had finished, I felt as though I was drunk—and I'd had lots of experience of feeling drunk. My speech was loud, my actions exaggerated, and I laughed and lolloped home, still tingling. Everything appeared strangely translucent. I could not stop talking to my friend about God. God was real; He had met me!

I had been wooed back to the Lord, drawn in by His gracious and gentle cords of love. He had sent several people into my life to speak a prophetic word. I had received several clear revelations and audible directions. But key to my return was finding an expression of Christianity that was biblically authentic, vigorous, and vital, not sterile as I had previously known—a church where God was immanent. Here there was real expectancy that He would speak and act and intervene. And He did. Here was a community of people who were not spectators at a one-man show, but partakers together in an encounter with God. Scripture was honored, sermons were twice as long as I expected. Worship in song to Christ was a priority rather than a prelude to the sermon. But the key to it all was the passionate pursuit of the presence of God on the part of the godly vicar and his team.

Although our evening services were occasionally marked by singing in tongues, this was within a strict framework of the liturgy, and the morning service was a rather conventional Anglican one. We were really a warm evangelical church, although a number of charismatics exercised the gifts in their home groups. The phenomena were somewhat incidental, although they were undeniable. But I had been given an assurance of faith and an experience of God that was glorious. More than that I sensed a growing desire to preach.

A year after I came back to Christ, a young minister named Charlie Cleverly came to our church to lead a weekend of renewal. On that Saturday morning everything changed, for the church and for me. After some worship Charlie spoke on renewal in the Spirit and a member of his team gave a testimony before reading Isaiah 43:19f.:

> *Behold I am doing a new thing, now it springs forth, do*
> *you not perceive it? I will make a way in the wilderness and*
> *rivers in the desert.... I give water in the wilderness, rivers*
> *in the desert, to give drink to my chosen people, the people*
> *whom I have formed for myself, that they might declare my*
> *praise. (ESV)*

At the end of the meeting Charlie told me that he felt led to pray for me. I went up to the front of the church and Charlie laid hands on me. Suddenly, unexpectedly, I fell to the floor. This had never happened in our church before.

As I lay on the floor, I was aware of wave after wave of God's love washing over me, like breakers on the seashore. I breathed in deeply, weeping with joy at God, who would visit even me. My chest felt as if it had a huge weight on it, the glory of the Lord upon me, but at the same time, anxieties and insecurities were being lifted off and God's tender Father's comfort was stilling my soul.

After perhaps fifteen minutes, during which Charlie had stood nearby praying for me, I stood up with the assistance of others. I extended a wobbly hand to Charlie and said, "Thanks very much," whereupon he simply said, "God hasn't finished," and again I went crashing to the floor. This time the sense was not of love being poured out, but of wave after wave of power filling me. Charlie began prophesying concerning my future and in particular about me becoming a preacher. Again I stood up, even more wobbly, and knew that I had been anointed and called forth to be a preacher.

Within a year, through a remarkable set of God-incidences, I was called out from secular employment to be a full-time evangelist. For the next eighteen months I traveled and preached in schools, churches, nursing homes, on the street, at house parties, and young people's meetings. Then the leadership of Holy Trinity, Nailsea, invited me to come and assist the senior curate, John Carter, in planting the new church. I was thrilled to join the team at the church where I had met the Lord just three years before. As parish evangelist I stayed and ministered there for three years, before going on to train for the ordained ministry in September 1991.

Much has happened in the years since then. Remarkably I am now working alongside Charlie Cleverly at St. Aldates, Oxford. But the lessons God inculcated in me through my early encounters with His Spirit have set me on a trajectory of expectancy that God is a God who is alive and well and active on planet earth. He is a God who comes, who speaks, who reveals, who touches, who heals, who delivers, who fills, who abides. The Christian life is one in which we can know intimately the Comforter with us, often through periods of great pain, filling our faltering faith with His fullness, equipping us for service. By the Spirit's revelation we may know what we believe from Scripture: that He is a Lover to His bride, a Father to His children, a King to His subjects, a Friend. He is the One who fills us with unspeakable joy and glory in His presence.

When I look back to the church experience of my childhood and teenage years, I can see the faith and faithfulness of my parents and some of those dear old saints. But for much of that time it seemed as if we were living religious lives and doing church according to memory, might, and the memorials of men. But the glory of God, the Spirit of Christ, had not departed. He was simply blowing where He willed. God was building His church by His Spirit all the time (Zech. 4:6). And for those who were keeping in step with the Spirit, rather than keeping in step with the past, there He was rebuilding His church, placing new wine in new wineskins. And wherever God's people were saying, "More, Lord, more of You, more of Your Spirit," there He was filling His house with glory greater than the former (Hag. 2:5–9).

I have sought to show that those who go most after God gain most from God. But it is also evident that those who go for God and gain from God are those through whom God gives Himself to the world. Those blessings received are turned outward into blessing others.

CHAPTER 5

PENTECOST: IN THE RIVER OVER OUR HEADS

O Holy Ghost whose temple I ...

Double in my heart thy flame.[1]

In the Old Testament the Israelites were no strangers to the Holy Spirit—or rather, the Holy Spirit was no stranger to them. However, the Spirit is never defined or systematized into doctrinal statements, but is recorded as the experience of the immanence of God in the lives of individuals. The Old Testament often speaks of the presence or felt activity of God in anthropomorphic terms: God's arm, hand, finger, face, glory, name, etc., drawing from human experience to symbolize the extension of His being, His felt presence, power, and action. In the same way, to speak of the Spirit of God is to speak of God's action among us, with us, and for us. The Spirit of God is His "specific and particular making of himself present."[2]

The Spirit of God, the *ruach* of God, like the wind, was elusive but dynamic. He had been active in the world since the very beginning. He was the dynamic source of creation, brooding over the waters, incubating creation into being (Gen. 1:2; Ps. 104:30). He was the breath, the source of life (Job 33:4). His presence would transform the wilderness into a paradise, a place of justice and righteousness (Isa. 32:15f.). He was the source of Bezalel's creative gifts for the building of the tabernacle (Ex. 31:23). He was the source of revelation and speech through the prophets (Num. 24:2; 2 Kings 2:9; 2 Sam. 23:2; Neh. 9:30; Ezek. 2—3; Dan. 4:8). The Spirit was the source of authority and power for leadership and kingship (Num. 11:25; 27:18; Judg. 6:34; 11:29; 15:14; 1 Sam. 10:6). The Spirit, though omnipresent (Ps. 139:7), could be grieved through sin and rebellion and His presence forfeited (1 Sam. 16:14; Ps. 51:11; Isa. 63:10).

THE MESSIAH AND THE SPIRIT

But the prophets looked forward to a day when God would send His deliverer, His Messiah, the Christ, the Anointed One of the Spirit, filled with wisdom, might, and compassion (Isa. 11:2; 61:1). They looked forward to a day when not only the great and the good, priests, prophets, kings, and judges would be filled with the Spirit, but when the Spirit would be poured out on all flesh (Joel 2:28), when God would place His Spirit within us, transforming hearts of stone into hearts of flesh, and conforming our lives to the righteousness of the law (Ezek. 11:19; 36:26). The Spirit's activity was one of anointing individuals to establish God's kingdom

(Israel), to bring revelation of God's character and will to the minds and through the mouths of His prophets, and to equip judges, kings, and priests for works of service. But these things were all partial and proleptic, anticipating a coming day when this elusive and often elitist[3] divine presence would bring the heavenly garden of Eden to all humankind.

When John the Baptist burst onto the scene and began preparing God's people for the coming of the King through repentance and baptism, he declared that the One for whom he was laying out the carpet, the One on whom he would see the Spirit descend and remain (John 1:32), was the Son of God, who would "baptize you with/in[4] the Holy Spirit and fire"[5] (Matt. 3:11). The Spirit-anointed One anoints with the Spirit. When Jesus came to be baptized, John the Baptist declared, "This is the One ..." Although Jesus was the divine eternal Son, conceived in Mary by the Holy Spirit (1:18–23), His ministry did not commence until the divine Holy Spirit anointed Him, in His humanity, at His baptism (3:16).

The Spirit prepared Jesus for ministry in the wilderness through victorious confrontation with the vicious demonic (Luke 4:1f.), and then the Spirit propels Him and empowers Him in ushering in the kingdom (vv. 14–21) and releasing people from the works of the Evil One. Jesus would give the Spirit without measure (John 3:34), the Spirit who is the means of regeneration (vv. 3–8), the means of satisfaction (4:1–15; 7:37f.) and true worship (John 4:24). Following Jesus' death, resurrection, and ascension, the Spirit would bring them counsel, comfort, assistance, and instruction (14:15–26). But this Spirit whom the disciples now know is "accompanying" them (Greek *par*), anointing their ministry (Matt. 10:1), will then be "in" (Greek *en*) them (John 14:17).

The Holy Spirit, who comes from the Father through Jesus (John 14:26; 16:7; 20:22) and who may be requested and received in great measure (John 3:34; Luke 11:9–13), is the Spirit of Truth (John 14:17; 16:13) who will bring to the world revelation of the truth of God's righteous judgment on sin (16:8) and a deeper revelation of the truth of Christ to His disciples. This Holy Spirit will empower the disciples in an ever-expanding witness to the truth of Christ (Luke 24:49; Acts 1:4, 8), but they are instructed to wait until they have received this promise of the Father. Even as they have been baptized in/with water by John, so shortly they will be baptized in/with the Holy Spirit (1:4–5).

The anticipation of the Old Testament, the prophecy of John the Baptist, and the promise of Jesus Christ burst forth on the day of Pentecost. Nothing would ever be the same again. Although the manifestations of the Spirit's visitation may not have been new (e.g., fire, wind, prophetic ecstatic utterance, etc.), what was new was the irrevocability of His coming, the intensity of His manifestation, and the intention of His appearing. Whereas previously He had anointed certain individuals for certain tasks, now He had come to integrate the believers into union with God, to institute a whole new people of God, and to inaugurate the new age of God.

This time it was specifically all about Jesus: applying the work of Christ at the cross to our lives in justification, regeneration, and sanctification (1 Cor. 6:11); presenting Christ to us as our Lord (12:3); glorifying Christ to us (John 16:13f.); immersing us into eternal mystical union with Christ (1 Cor. 12:13); anointing us as witnesses to the death, resurrection, ascension, return, and reign of King Jesus (Acts 1:8) with signs following (Rom. 15:19); transforming our sinful natures into holy conformity with Christ (2 Cor. 3:17f.; Gal. 5:16f.); preparing us as the bride for Christ's return (Gal. 5:5; Rev. 22:17) as we wait in joy, peace, and hope (Rom. 15:13).

ACTS 2: PENTECOST, IN THE DAY OF THY POWER

Jerusalem was pregnant and pulsating with several hundred thousand[6] Jewish pilgrims and proselytes (converts to Judaism) who had traveled from throughout the Roman Empire and Greek-speaking world to celebrate this major religious festival. Pentecost was so called because it fell on the fiftieth day[7] after the presentation of the first sheaf to be reaped from the barley harvest.[8] It was also termed the "feast of weeks" (Ex. 34:22), or the day of the "firstfruits" (Num. 28:26; Ex. 23:16), because on that day the firstfruits of the wheat harvest were presented to God. It later became the occasion for celebrating the giving of the law to Moses at Sinai (19:1) due to that event's general proximity to the first Passover and also the giving of the covenant to Noah (Gen. 9; Jubilees 6).

So on this day, when pilgrims have gathered from around the Empire to celebrate God's provision of the firstfruits of harvest, when they commemorate God's provision of the old covenants through Moses and Noah, God chooses to come with the firstfruits of the age of the Spirit and establish a new covenant, written not on tablets of stone but on people's hearts. Pentecost represented the birthday of God's old covenant people, Israel, and it would now represent the birthday of God's new covenant people, the church. The first is not negated, but consummated in the second. Even as those first pilgrims at Pentecost came there to give thanks for God's provision of the harvest and the law, so we must constantly come back to that first Pentecost, giving thanks for the firstfruits of the Spirit's outpouring, and realign ourselves with that plumb line of God's action.

The Pentecost coming of the Spirit was prophesied

The major Old Testament prophets, writing between 600 and 700 BC (Isa. 44:3f.; Jer. 31:33; Ezek. 11:19; 36:26), had all prophesied that there would be a new work of God, by the Spirit outpoured, consecrating God's people to Himself, writing His law on their hearts. Even earlier (c. 800 BC), the prophet Joel had seen and spoken of a day when God would pour out His Spirit on all flesh, not just on Israel's elite. John the Baptist (Luke 3:16) had prophesied that the Christ would baptize them by the Holy Spirit (*pneuma*) and fire (*pur*), and had said that Jesus was the One. Jesus had repeatedly spoken to His disciples of His and the Father's sending of the promised Holy Spirit, for whom they were to wait before witnessing to His resurrection (Luke 24:49; Acts 1:4).

Isaiah foretold, "Under [God's] glory a fire will be kindled. Like a burning flame. And the light of Israel will become a fire and His Holy One a flame burning and devouring its thorns and briars in a single day" (10:16b). As these disciples are gathered together, expectantly and obediently in prayer (Acts 1:14), suddenly they hear a sound like a mighty wind (*pneuma*) filling the whole house, and what seem to be (i.e., not actual) tongues of fire (*pur*) appeared and divided and rested on each one.[9]

Incidentally a bishop's mitre (headpiece) is always shaped like a tongue to remind the church that she (represented by the bishop) is brought to birth in the fire of the Spirit's presence. After all, a Christian is a person who has caught fire from God's manifest, consuming, purging presence. As Kierkegaard states so powerfully, "Christianity is incendiarism; Christianity is fire setting; a Christian is a person set on fire."[10] The psalmist says, "God makes the winds His messengers and His servants flames of fire" (Ps. 104:4). Pentecost shows that God sends His fire to make His messengers. The Scottish prophet James Stuart Stewart declared, "When all is said and done, the supreme need of the Church is the same in the 20th century as in the first—it is men on fire for Christ. I beg you do not commit the fearful blunder of dampening down that flame."[11] Pentecost is God sending that fire to fill His church with power to speak prophetically of His Son. "Do not quench the Spirit" (1 Thess. 5:19). We need to pray with Charles Wesley:

> *O Thou who camest from above,*
> *The pure celestial fire to impart,*
> *Kindle a flame of sacred love,*
> *On the mean altar of my heart.*
> *There, let it for Thy glory burn,*
> *With inextinguishable blaze,*
> *And trembling to its source return*
> *In humble prayer and fervent praise.*
> *Jesus confirm my heart's desire,*
> *To work and speak and think for Thee,*

Still let me guard the Holy Fire,
And still stir up Thy gift in me.

When I applied to be the Oxford Pastorate Chaplain in 1998, the application requested the chaplain be someone "ablaze with the love of Christ." I wrote that this was something I longed to be. In many respects this book is autobiographical, showing the paths I have followed in search of being set ablaze by the love of and love for Christ. George Whitefield asked, "What is a Christian without a Holy warmth?"

Augustine prayed, "O love ever burning and never extinguished, caritas, My God. Set me on fire." There is a Puritan prayer that asks, "Oh that I could be a flame of fire in thy service—always burning out in one continual blaze." I have come to believe that we will ignite to the extent that we delight in God. As we draw near to that burning bush, that pillar of fire, then we too will catch fire. Love for Him, love from Him welcomes us into the blaze of God.

When this happens to the disciples, when the Holy Spirit fills them, they begin to speak in languages other than their own, as the Spirit takes hold of their mouths, and they cannot help praising God. They spill out onto the streets, declaring the wonders of God, and crowds of pilgrims are drawn to them, somewhat bemused by this overt, public ecstatic behavior. Peter stands forward and, addressing the crowd, says, "This is that which the prophet Joel announced" (Acts 2:16)—this is the fulfillment of the prophetic promise that in the last days God will pour out His Holy Spirit on all flesh.

God's Spirit did not just fall out of heaven to earth one day, but rather here was God's long-awaited plan to visit, vitalize, and vocalize

His church and through them the world. Centuries of expectation and anticipation find their realization in the church of Christ born anew of the Spirit from above (John 3). What the prophets foresaw through a mirror dimly and foretold, here finds its fulfillment. What they saw, we savor. God is a God who speaks and shows, who says what He means and does what He says.

At the heart of this weight of prophecy is a personal indwelling life in the Spirit of God. What was prophesied was not a once-only event for those 120 people on the day of Pentecost, but a personal baptism of the Spirit, a union of the saved human soul with God, for all who would believe in Christ Jesus. This Pentecost was the first, but it was not the last. On that day when the Jewish people celebrated the "firstfruits of the harvest," we see the firstfruits of the reception of the Spirit.

The Pentecost coming of the Spirit was prophetic

Not only is God fulfilling His promise, but the manner and the mode in which He does this is pregnant with prophetic meaning. Pentecost is not simply God keeping His word, but God speaking a word.

First, Pentecost was prophetic in that it saw the gift of the Spirit inaugurating God's new covenant with humankind. The sending of the Spirit on Pentecost, the day of commemoration for the giving of the Noahic and Mosaic covenants, was no accident. It was divinely orchestrated and meticulously executed in its timing. Even as Christ came to die at Passover—the true fulfillment of what that thirteen-hundred-year-old meal of deliverance symbolized, so too the Spirit coming on this Pentecost day was the fulfillment of that Jewish day of thanksgiving for God's gracious provision of a harvest and of the giving of the covenants of grace that had framed God's people.[12] By coming on this day, God's seal of the Spirit looks backward and declares "yes" to these old promises and provisions, while at the same time looking forward and heralding the day of "new beginnings," new thanksgivings for these new provisions, a new birth, a new covenant, a new people.

Second, Pentecost was prophetic in that it showed the gift of the Spirit had come to all. In the Old Testament the Spirit's activity was marked by a particularity—anointing very few indeed, usually just a handful in any one era, namely its princes, priests, and prophets. From a distance people may have watched the privileged few, and wondered what it was like to know the anointing of the Spirit, but such an encounter, experience, and equipping was unavailable to the ordinary Israelite and only given to those elite with a specific task in hand, be it prophesying, ruling, or defeating Israel's enemies. But at Pentecost everything changes. In Acts 2:1–4 there is an obvious stress on the inclusive nature of this event and experience. All (i.e., the believers in Christ) were together in one place, the Spirit as tongues of fire came and rested on each one of them, they were all filled with the Spirit and began to speak in other languages.

Peter, drawing on Joel, underlines the inclusivity of this experience. Quoting Joel, he says, "I will pour out My Spirit on all flesh" (Acts 2:17), and then he defines this: "Your sons and your daughters will prophesy, your young men shall see visions and your old men dream dreams; even on My slaves [men and women in those days] I will pour out My Spirit …" He is making the point that this outpouring of the Spirit is not racist ("all flesh"), not sexist ("sons and daughters"), not ageist ("young men and old men"), and not elitist ("male and female slaves").[13]

Pentecost is the great equalizer and the great social transformer. The gift of the Spirit brings actual communion with God and authentic communism among humankind.

The great Pentecostal movement of the twentieth century, which has now grown to four hundred million, began with a remarkable outpouring of the Holy Spirit on a group of believers who had been seeking God for "more." One key feature in its early days was its radical racial and social integration, unknown in the mainline denominations. Indeed, one of the reasons why it initially had so many detractors was that it annulled the previous fixed barriers of race, sex, and class. In the barn in Azusa Street where it all began in 1906 under the ministry of the African-American pastor William J. Seymour, it was said that "the color line was washed away in the blood" of Jesus.[14] Indeed, not only the color line but also the gender, race, and class lines were washed away as thousands from all over the world and from every conceivable background came together and drank of the outpouring of God's river. In the very first issues of the paper "The Apostolic Faith," which Seymour produced in 1907 to articulate and promulgate this revival, he emphasized how the Spirit establishes a reconciliation, unity, and equality across social, racial, or gender spectrums: "The people are all melted together ... made one lump, one bread, all one body in Christ Jesus. There is no Jew or Gentile, bond or free, in the Azusa Street Mission ... He is no respecter of persons or places."[15]

Third, Pentecost was prophetic in demonstrating that Jesus is Lord. Peter's sermon explaining this event does not concern itself with the existential experience or the observable phenomena. What matters is not so much the manner of the Spirit's coming but the meaning. And it means only one thing: that this fulfillment of Old Testament Scripture is proof that Jesus is the exalted King (Acts 2:22–36).

Peter presents a wonderfully fulsome yet succinct Christology:

- v. 22a: Jesus' history—"of Nazareth"
- v. 22b: Jesus' ministry—"attested by God with mighty works, signs, and wonders"
- v. 23a: Jesus' destiny—"according to God's definite plan and foreknowledge"
- v. 23b: Jesus' agony—"you crucified and killed Him by the hands of lawless men"
- v. 24: Jesus' victory—"God raised Him up, loosing the pangs of death"
- vv. 25f.: Jesus' prophecy—"David foretold the resurrection of God's Holy One"
- vv. 33f.: Jesus' glory—"resurrected, exalted, seated at God's right hand"
- v. 33: Jesus' bounty—"received the promise of the Father and poured it out on us"
- v. 34: Jesus' sovereignty—"The Lord said to my Lord, sit at my right hand"

Three times Peter speaks of "this thing" (*touto*, vv. 14, 16, 33), referring to these Pentecost events, and three times he speaks of "this person" (*touton*, vv. 23, 32, 36), referring to the Lord Jesus. This thing that Jesus' disciples are experiencing, and that the crowds are witnessing, is itself a witness to this person Jesus (vv. 22–36). The Spirit of God, poured out upon the disciples of Jesus, can mean only one thing: that this Jesus whom they rejected and crucified, who was raised from the dead and ascended into heaven, has been exalted to the Father's right hand and has received from God, and poured out for all to see today, the promised gift of the Holy Spirit (vv. 32–33).

Watchman Nee beautifully illustrated this point by referring analogously to the story of Joseph and his elderly father Jacob (Gen. 45).[16] Jacob thought that Joseph was dead and mourned the loss of his dearest son. When the brothers tried to convince him that they had seen him alive, his heart was numb and unbelieving (v. 26). But Joseph was alive, and sent wagons laden with bountiful gifts to collect his father. When he saw the caravan of wagons, Jacob's spirit revived, and he said, "'Tis enough, my son is alive." Watchman Nee says that the coming of the Holy Spirit is like the sending ahead of the bountifully laden wagons to bestow on us great gifts and to bring us back to Christ.

The observable sending of the Spirit to the disciples of Christ is a tangible proof of their claim that Jesus is risen from the dead and ascended to the right hand of the Father. Peter's argument is something of a reasoned apologetic defense of Christ. But the fact of the Spirit's coming is not only evidential of Christ's lordship. When He encounters the human spirit, there is an existential witness to Jesus' divinity. The Holy Spirit writes on our spirit and articulates through our mouth that "Jesus is Lord" (1 Cor. 12:2f.).

Following John Wesley's anointing with the Spirit, bringing the "strange warming" of his heart as he heard the Moravians at Aldersgate preaching from Luther's preface to his commentary on

Romans, he wrote in his diary the following day, May 25, 1738, that the moment he awoke, "'Jesus Master' was in my heart and in my mouth …"[17] The Spirit will always shine the spotlight on Christ—He will always put Christ center stage and manifest Christ in His divine lordship. Jonathan Edwards said, "God has had it in his heart from all eternity to glorify his dear Son, and there are special seasons which he appoints to that end. These are times of remarkable outpouring of his Spirit to advance his kingdom. Such is a day of power." Such was the day of Pentecost, a day in which the Spirit came and glorified Christ.

The Pentecost coming of the Spirit made prophets

The streets were swarming with pilgrims who had come in part to celebrate the covenant God had given through the greatest Old Testament prophet, Moses. Moses on one occasion declared, "I would that all God's people were prophets" (Num. 11:29). At Pentecost his desire became a reality. "All of them were filled with the Holy Spirit and began to speak in other tongues as the Spirit gave utterance" (Acts 2:4). The multitude was attracted and amazed (v. 6) because they heard these Galileans (presumably their strong northern accent gave them away) "declaring in our own tongues the mighty wonders of God" (v. 8). When Peter refers to Joel to make sense of this event, he refers to Joel's prophetic promise that an evidence of the Spirit's outpouring on all flesh would be that the "sons and daughters" and "male and female slaves" would "prophesy" (vv. 17–18). The Reformation emphasizes the priesthood of all believers. While this is true (1 Peter 2:5; Rev. 5:10), Pentecost actually points to the prophethood of all believers.[18]

The Holy Spirit is a revealing and speaking Spirit. In the Old Testament economy, when He came upon individuals they prophesied (Num. 11:24f.; 1 Sam. 10:6; Ezek. 2—3). In the New Testament, Luke makes this direct link between the anointing or filling with the Spirit and revelatory prophetic speech with Elizabeth (Luke 1:41), Zechariah (v. 67), Simeon (2:27f.), and preeminently Jesus Himself (Lk. 4:18). The Holy Spirit is a prophetic Spirit. He is garrulous, and with the occasional exceptions where being Spirit filled was for an anointing for war (Othniel in Judg. 3; Samson in Judg. 15) or artistic design (Bezalel in Ex. 31), the other incidents all involve inspired speech of some form.

The Spirit-filled believer is rarely silent. Peter, who would later write concerning the Old Testament authors, "Men spoke from God as they were carried along by the Holy Spirit" (2 Peter 1:21 NIV), was emboldened by the Spirit to preach to the crowds. Remember, this was the Peter who denied Jesus three times, but now, anointed by the Holy Spirit, he is on fire and preaches fearlessly and fiercely. Chadwick notes, "When our Fathers glowed with fires kindled in the soul they gave vent in noise. The modern way is to be still."[19] In the creeds one of the few predicates attached to the Spirit is that "He has spoken through the prophets." Only occasionally foretelling, usually the Spirit comes for the purpose of forthtelling the wonders of God. He brings revelation of God, but this is not for personal consumption: Filled with the Spirit, they spilled out onto the streets. The Holy Spirit will always produce speech to God's glory through the recipient, but that is not simply personal truth—it is public truth (1 Cor. 12:2). Far from observing polite social conventions, these Spirit-filled individuals make such a noise that they interrupt the other worshippers at the temple. And the response? Some mused (Acts 2:12), "What does this mean?" Some mocked (v. 13), "They must be drunk!" But some were moved (v. 37), "Cut to the heart, they asked: What must we do to be saved? Three thousand were added to their number that day" (v. 41).

The famous evangelist and revivalist Charles Finney tells of a period in his early ministry when there was much verbal and even physical objection to what he was doing. Having spent the afternoon in prayer in the woods with a friend, he entered the meeting house and a large crowd gathered to hear him. People left their games on the village green and shopkeepers closed up. The room was packed to the gills. Finney, without thought of notes or sermon preparation, records what happened:

> *The Spirit of God came upon me with such power that it was like opening up a battery [a row of cannons] upon them. For more than an hour the Word of God came through me to them in a manner that I could see was carrying all before it. It was a fire, and as a hammer breaking upon the rock, and as the sword that was piercing to the dividing of soul and spirit.*[20]

The intense opposition melted away under the anointing of God, with many falling under deep conviction of sin and being brought to repentance. Note the crucial interplay between Word and Spirit in Finney's testimony, pairing the Spirit of God and the Word of God, using metaphors together of fire (Spirit) and sword/hammer (Word).

PENTECOST—POWER FOR WITNESS

K. P. Yohanan is the apostolic figure and founder of Gospel for Asia, a pioneering church-planting and frontline missionary organization that, through its thirty-one colleges, has equipped and sent out ten thousand evangelists into the unreached people groups of Asia, planting ten new churches every day. In his book *Revolution in World Missions*, Yohanan remarked on his first impressions of his visit to America (and his observations hold true for the UK): "I found that believers are ready to get involved in almost any activity which looks spiritual but allows them to escape their responsibility to the gospel."[21]

He noted that the average American has four Bibles, while 80 percent of the world's population does not own one. In the States there is one Christian worker for every 230 people, while the unreached have one missionary per 500,000. There are five thousand Christian bookstores, hundreds of Christian magazines, papers, radio stations, and television programs, but, says Yohanan, "The saddest observation is that little, if any, of this media is designed to reach unbelievers. Almost all is entertainment for saints."

The Holy Spirit did not come for our entertainment or excitement, but for our empowerment for evangelism. He filled the church that the church might fill the world. At the heart of that first Pentecost outpouring, and of every subsequent visitation from on high, is the receiving of power to witness to Christ (Acts 1:8). Yes, the Spirit comes to bring us the actuality and assurance of salvation; yes, the Spirit comes to bring us the knowledge of our adoption; yes, the Spirit comes to inculcate in us the life and character of Christ; yes, the Spirit comes to impart the intimacy and glory of God to us; yes, the Spirit comes to impart gifts for the building up and blessing of the body of Christ; but power from on high to point to the One seated on high is among the preeminent purposes of Pentecost. Sadly this divine priority has often become a mere footnote in the life of the church. At times, we have been more interested in the inward feelings and phenomena associated with the Spirit's coming than in His focus to propel us outward to a godless, hopeless, lightless world where eighty thousand die daily without Christ.

The experience of the Spirit, if authentic, will always have an exocentric impulse—propelling us from that experience outward to Christ and the world. Karl Barth powerfully emphasizes this role of the Spirit:

> *Those who accept the witness of the Spirit cannot tarry*
> *with him as such. There can be no abstract receiving and*
> *possessing of the Holy Spirit. There can be no self-moved and*
> *self-resting life in the Spirit, no self-sufficient spiritual status.*
> *The witness of the Holy Spirit does not have itself either as its*
> *origin or its goal.*[22]

The Holy Spirit comes to make Christ known to us as Savior and Lord, and to make Christ known through us to the world as its Savior and Lord.

The outstanding evangelist Brother Yun of China recalls in his biographical account[23] how one day he was reading and meditating on Acts 1:8, "You will receive power when the Holy Spirit comes upon you, and you will be My witnesses...." Yun recalls,

*I wasn't sure who the Holy Spirit was. I ran and asked my
mother. She couldn't explain. She simply said, "… Why don't
you pray and ask God for the Holy Spirit just like you prayed
for your Bible?"… I prayed to the Lord, "I need the power of
the Holy Spirit. I am willing to be your witness." After the
prayer God's Spirit of joy fell upon me. A deep revelation of
God's love and presence flooded my being. I'd never enjoyed
singing before but many new songs of worship flowed from my
lips. They were words I had never learned before. Later I wrote
them down. These songs are still sung in the Chinese house
churches to this day.*

From that moment on, Yun began to witness to Christ with
extraordinary power and fruitfulness. He later wrote, "Even though I
was a teenager, the Lord enabled me to lead more than two thousand
people to Jesus in my first year as a Christian."[24]

In Acts 1:6 the disciples ask Jesus whether at this time He
will restore the kingdom to Israel. They were still thinking materially and nationally, and perhaps even a little selfishly (Luke 9:46;
Matt. 20:21). As F. F. Bruce says, "This present question appears to
have been the last flicker of their former burning expectation of an
imminent theocracy with themselves as its chief executives."[25] Jesus
quickly and sharply puts them right. They are interested in what
Jesus will do, and in what they might gain from it; Jesus is interested
in what they will do and what the world will gain. They are interested
in Israel; Jesus is interested in the world. They are concerned with
issues over which the Father has drawn a veil. How often the church
is sidetracked from her divine vocation by failing to understand her

responsibilities, by a parochial egocentricity, and by a concern with issues that do not concern her.

In Acts 1:8, Jesus' "but" refocuses their attention to the important issue at hand. He promises an extraordinary encounter—"the Holy Spirit will come upon you," an explosive equipping—"you will receive power," and an expansive evangelism—"you will be My witnesses in Jerusalem, Judea, Samaria, to the ends of the earth."

These three clearly identifiable clauses interlock into one indivisible expectation and instruction. The experience is to empower us to evangelize. This is an experience of God directed toward witnessing to Christ. This is an empowering directed toward witnessing to Christ. This witnessing to Christ is impossible without the experience of empowering. The church is full of those who want experiences of God coming upon them for their own sake, divorced from witness; the church is full of those who want God's power for existential or empire-building purposes; the church is full of those who have a vision for the nations but no means and often no message to take them there.[26] But the promised Pentecost experience is preeminently power to proclaim Christ. Receiving the promise, *pro-mittere* (Acts 1:4), releases the mission, *mittere* (v. 8).[27]

Of note here is the Roman Catholic reflection on the experience of Pentecost and the charismatic renewal movement that began sweeping Catholicism in the 1970s. Cardinal Suenens commissioned a study by an international team of theologians at Malines on the causes, content, and questions that needed to be asked of the movement. The findings were favorable and the commission's published report was summed up in the powerful and pointed title, "Towards a New Pentecost for a New Evangelisation." The report states,

> *The experience of the power of the Holy Spirit effects a radical inner conversion and a deep transformation ... The Holy Spirit is experienced as the power to serve and witness, to preach the gospel in word and deed with the manifestation of power which moves to faith and arouses faith.*

It claims that a major strength of charismatic renewal is in the area of evangelization.[28] "To receive the Spirit is to be moved and to move others to the recognition that Jesus is Lord" (1 Cor. 12:3).

In Acts 13:2–4 we meet the Holy Spirit speaking to the Antioch believers, setting Barnabas and Saul apart and sending them out on apostolic mission. They do not celebrate their experience of the Spirit or their hearing of the Spirit—they simply obey the Spirit and go. The Spirit is not for their entertainment, but for their empowerment for witness. How terrible it is when the church desires an experience of the Holy Spirit for its own sake, a self-indulgence with no intention to engage in mission.

Hendrikus Berkhof says, "Pentecost (Acts 2) is both the birth of the Church and the birth of Missions. All of Acts narrates the earliest history of the Church as mission history."[29] The distinguished missionary and writer on the life in the Spirit Andrew Murray has pointedly stated, "No one may expect to be filled with the Spirit if he is not willing to be used in missions."[30] We must be careful not to pray "Come Holy Spirit" unless we are prepared to "Go with the Holy Spirit."

FRUIT AND FAITHFULNESS, NOT PHENOMENA

Often when the Spirit comes, there are associated phenomena. Surely we cannot expect Almighty God to visit us, saturate us, supernaturally transform and equip us, while we remain emotionally and physically like marble? The observers at Pentecost thought the people had been drinking too much new wine (Acts 2:13). Why? This was a major religious festival when people were excited and expectant about the coming of their Messiah. It would not have been unusual to have people in public praising God—one only has to visit Jerusalem during a festival or Shabbat to see groups of Jewish men dancing and singing in public. Was the accusation that they were drunk rooted in other phenomena associated with drunkenness, such as staggering, falling, or loudness? Peter spoke of them "seeing and hearing" (v. 33) the effect of the coming of the Spirit. In Acts 8:18, Simon Magus, when he saw the Spirit was given at the laying on of hands, sought to buy this power to enable him also to work such an effect. What did he see? Was it just people speaking in tongues? Presumably then Scripture would have stated, "When he heard them speak in tongues as the Spirit came ..." Could it be that under the anointing they were acting as if drunk?

Physical phenomena accompanying the visitation of the Spirit are a hallmark of every revival, including the Great Awakening, the Evangelical Awakening, and the Pentecostal outpouring. Swooning, crying out, shuddering, falling, lying prostrate, and motionless for some hours—all are recorded and documented features of revival. Charismatics often point out that when the Spirit comes individuals can shake, laugh, cry, fall, roll around, jump, find their hands trembling, their eyelids fluttering, and so on. Psychologists may see these as biochemically induced reactions—endorphins and other neurotransmitters pumping round the brain, overactivating brain cells and eliciting unusual physical manifestations.

Whatever the cause, whatever the reaction, whatever the manifestation, the phenomena are somewhat unimportant. We are not to seek such things and we are not to restrict such things. We are to seek the Holy Spirit and look for the fruit of changed and empowered lives. We must not be distracted or abstracted by phenomena, either as critics or as thrill-seekers. Let us press beyond these trimmings for God Himself—any encounter with God must be judged on its fruit and faithfulness, never on mere feelings or phenomena. These are like smoke that accompanies fire—but it is the fire we seek.

Here, then, is the divine economy: The Father sent the Son, the Father and the Son sent the Spirit, and the Spirit sends the church. Those who will not go will never know the anointing of the Spirit or the heart of God. Those who claim to have been filled with the Spirit but do not overflow in witness are deceiving themselves. They know nothing of "Calvary love" or "Pentecost fire."

But when the Spirit descends upon a people or a person, He also sends them.

That was the experience of the Moravian community in the early eighteenth century.[31] They were a group of refugees who were taken in and settled on the estates of Count Zinzendorf, a man marked by an intense passion for Jesus and for making Him known. This community subsequently knew a remarkable outpouring of the Holy

Spirit and boldly manifested His character and His gifts. But mission was the mark of their Pentecost. Burdened with God's heart, to make Christ known among nations where He was not known, they poured themselves out in prayer, support, financing, and the sending of pioneering missionaries to such diverse places as the West Indies, Greenland, South Africa, Labrador, and England, where they lit a flame in John Wesley, who went on to light a flame throughout England.

This is the Spirit of Pentecost—a Spirit of power for witnessing to Christ. That was what they experienced that first Pentecost when they declared the praises of God, and Peter preached to the crowds, seeing three thousand saved. That is the spreading flame throughout Acts as the Spirit anoints, equips, and expels missionaries from Jerusalem, Judea, Samaria, and the uttermost ends of the earth. That is the testimony we see even on the lips of those who oppose the church (Acts 19:26; 24:5). In one generation the gospel has spread the length and breadth of the Roman Empire. Within three hundred years that very Roman Empire that killed Christ and persecuted the church surrenders to Christ.

As the church historian Professor Henry Chadwick says, in three centuries, "Christian missionaries of spiritual but no great intellectual power, had enabled the gospel to take hold of the entire Roman Empire, Persia, Armenia, Scythia and even Great Britain."[32] They had spiritual but no great intellectual power (Acts 4:13). That, of course, is the testimony of the apostle Paul. Although highly educated and intellectually gifted, personally tutored at the feet of the great scholar Gamaliel (Acts 22:3), in his ministry Paul relied not on his education but on his divine unction. He tells us that when he visited Corinth, "I was with you in weakness, fear and trembling, and my speech and my message were not in plausible words of wisdom but in a demonstration of the Spirit and of power, that your faith might not rest in the wisdom of men but in the power of God" (1 Cor. 2:1f.).

In my experience the church has been more eager to see its ministers conferred with degrees than with the power of God. But if we are not simply to resist the attrition of the world, the flesh, and the Devil, but are actually to make inroads in their domain, extending the kingdom of God in the lives of individuals and transforming society, then what we need are not vicars in church sporting academic hoods but ministers clothed with tongues of fire. Now I am no anti-intellectual—I hold undergraduate and research degrees in theology—but these are no substitute for filling with the Spirit. The church does not need more academic degrees; she needs heating up by degree—more fire that she might be ablaze by the Spirit (Rom. 12:11), rather than, as so often, being tepid (Rev. 3:15).

In Peter Brierley's 1998 statistical survey of English churches, he noted that in real terms, over two thousand people leave the church each week. The evangelical churches are declining in real terms at a rate that is three times slower than nonevangelicals, but any decline is an affront to Pentecost, which envisaged ever-increasing growth from Jerusalem, Judea, Samaria, and so on.

Archbishop Carey, commenting on this, said, "If our response to this crisis does not lead us to Christ, it will surely end in the decline for our churches today … in some sections of the Western Church we are bleeding to death!"[33]

We are faced with a choice—revival or survival. Revival is where Pentecost in a church spills out into the streets. That is what happened in Acts 2, when three thousand were added to the church in one day. Oh, for a logistical nightmare like that! That is what happens in every revival: The Spirit fills the members of the church, who spill onto the streets, impacting communities with the life-giving message of Christ. In the Welsh Revival, in the first six months, it was estimated that a hundred thousand converts were won, and within one year a third of the population were registered communicant members of churches. Before the church can fill the world, God the Spirit must come and fill her. She needs to visit Pentecost. But in order to fill the church, the Spirit needs to fill you. Samuel Chadwick says, "That which happened at Pentecost is the biggest thing that ever happened. And now the biggest question of all is—has it happened to you and me?"[34]

So how do we prepare for, anticipate, and bring forth Pentecost in ourselves, our families, and our churches? For this we must look to Scripture, to Christ, and to the early church.

CLEARING THE PATH FOR PENTECOST

Step 1—Repentance

John baptized as a symbolic washing away of sins for those who embraced the kingdom, preparing for the King who would immerse them in the Spirit (Matt. 3:11). Jesus, the Son of Man, is baptized not only to legitimize John's ministry, but primarily as the representative of humanity. He is not renouncing and washing away His own sin, for He is sinless, but He does so symbolically and representatively on our behalf. Having said this yes to repentance, He Himself receives the Holy Spirit, who descends upon Him as a dove (v. 16). In this example we see that the Spirit comes to the repentant. In Acts 1:14 we read that the disciples devoted themselves to prayer. Scripture places a veil over the content of their prayers, but as anyone who prays knows, the longer we spend in prayer, drawing near to God, the more we are aware of our own sin, rebellion, unbelief, and need of God's grace. If we could hear their prayers in that upper room, as they await the visitation of the Spirit, I suspect we would hear strong cries of confession and see a floor wet with their tears.

Peter, in his Pentecost address, responds to the convicted listeners by telling them to repent and be baptized in Jesus' name. This confession and renunciation of sin, joined to an identification with and reception of Christ as Lord, will bring them the gift of the Spirit. This promise of the Holy Spirit (Acts 2:33, 38) is for them, their children, and for all who are far off. The Spirit comes to the repentant.

In England we call Pentecost "Whit Sunday," an old English shortening of "White Sunday." This stems from the time when Pentecost, like Easter, was a key occasion for baptism, and the candidates would come up out of the water and be clothed in white, symbolizing sins washed white as snow in the baptismal waters. I love that identification of Pentecost with White Sunday—the day of baptismal repentance and identification with Christ in His death.

The coming of the Spirit is also often coupled with a conviction of sin, righteousness, and judgment (John 16:8). The holy unearths the unholy. If we seek Him and respond to Him, He will clean our sin away, but if we continue in sin, He will keep His distance. When David repented following his sin over Bathsheba and Uriah, he implored the Lord not to remove him from His presence or take the Holy Spirit from him (Ps. 51:11). His unholy acts forfeited the sense of the presence of the Holy Spirit. While I do not believe that as Christians we can ever lose that seal of ownership (Eph. 1:13), by sin we may grieve and offend His presence within us. When individuals come to me and ask how they can know more of the power of the Holy Spirit, or if they share that they have lost the intimacy they once knew with Him, I will always try to discover whether there is unconfessed sin. The Holy Spirit will not anoint, indeed will avoid, marked unholiness (1 Cor. 3:16; 6:19; Eph. 4:30; Gal. 5). Not that our repentance makes us holy, but it is an invitation and preparation for the Holy Spirit to come and conform us into His likeness.

Step 2—Obedience

A visitation of the Spirit is known by those who say yes to God. Jesus said to the disciples, "Do not leave Jerusalem, but wait for the gift my Father promised" (Acts 1:4 NIV). They returned to Jerusalem and did just what the Lord asked of them. Had they gone off witnessing without this anointing, they would have done it in their own strength, which was very little, and they would have been singularly ineffective. But in obedience to Christ's command, they waited and prayed, and then the Spirit came. Later Peter could talk about "the Holy Spirit God gives to those who are obedient to Him" (5:32).

One commentator on the Sialkot revival in the early years of the twentieth century wrote that there are two conditions for God to use us in revival to win souls—obedience and purity. "Obedience in everything, even in the least, surrendering up our wills and taking the will of God."[35]

Samson was anointed by the Spirit of God to overcome the enemies of Israel (Judg. 14:6, 19; 15:14). When he gives Delilah the secrets of his strength (Judg. 16) and she cuts off his hair, his strength evaporates. Now his strength was not in the hair itself—that would be magic. But the hair symbolized his consecration and separation to God, and in this lay his anointing. To keep his hair long came as a command from God (13:4) and as long as he was faithful and obedient to this divine decree, he knew the Spirit's anointing. Samson's sin was not that he was gullible, but that he was sinful—immorality with a pagan prostitute and a disregard for God's gift cost him the anointing.

Similarly King Saul forfeited the anointing of the Spirit through his willful disobedience. Although he claimed to have performed the commandment of the Lord, Samuel's strong rebuke to Saul was that he had offered sacrifices, rather than obey God's command. Saul, who had been a Spirit-anointed prophet of the Lord, from that day on lost the anointing of the Spirit (1 Sam. 15:19–22; 16:14; 18:12). God replaced Saul with David, "a man after My own heart, who will do all My will" (Acts 13:22).

Jesus made it unequivocally plain that obedience and anointing go hand in hand. "If you love Me you will keep My commandment, and I will ask the Father to give you another Helper, to be with you for ever, even the Spirit of truth" (John 14:15–17). Let us not miss this sequitur: Reception of the Spirit follows faithful response to Christ's commands.

If we are seeking more of God's Holy Spirit power and presence in our lives, we need to ask ourselves: Am I doing everything God wants of me? Is there a particular thing He has asked me to do that I am hesitating about or refusing? If so, be quick: Repent, and obey. Obedience is a key that unlocks the door to every deep spiritual experience.

Step 3—Unity

The psalmist writes, "How good and pleasant it is when brothers live together in unity. It is like the precious oil on the head, running down on the beard of Aaron … for there the Lord has commanded blessing and life for ever more" (Ps. 133:1–3). Anointing with oil was performed on priests, prophets, and kings, and symbolized a setting apart and a sealing and anointing for the call at hand, by the Holy Spirit (Lev. 21:10; 1 Sam. 10:1, 6; 16:13; 1 Kings 19:16; 2 Kings 9:1f.).[36] The psalmist is celebrating the reality that when brothers dwell in harmony and unity, there the blessing of God is not simply a consequence but specifically a "command" of God.

Unity among the disciples was the weighty burden of Jesus' heart cry to His Father at the Last Supper. He prayed "that they may be one," even as God in His triune individual but indivisible persons is one (John 17:11, 21–23). But why is this oneness so important, so urgent, so incumbent upon Him? Jesus prays (v. 20) for the Twelve and for all who will believe through their word in order that[37] they may "be one," modeling the "oneness" in the Godhead, in order that "they also may be in Us," in order that "the world might believe that God sent [Jesus]." Leon Morris rightly comments, "In other words, the unity for which he prays is to lead to a fuller experience of the Father and the Son. And this in turn will have the further consequences that the world may believe."[38]

But what is this "fuller experience"? How is this indwelling in God (John 17:21) and indwelling of God (v. 23) achieved? It is achieved by none other than the anointing of the Holy Spirit, who unites us to Christ and who immerses us in the life of God (14:17; 1 John 2:27; John 17:23, 26). The Spirit is God in us who places us with God. It is not the communal oneness itself that establishes belief; it is the apostolic preaching of the "Word" (v. 20b) that speaks the why and wherefore of God's sending of His Son (v. 21c). But it is that community of the people of God, through communion with God, made possible by the Spirit of God that creates a context for the reception of the Word of Christ. This is Christ's prayer for a threefold cord—unity within the church, intimacy with God, and efficacy in witness. The "word" is hardly heard when the witnesses are not one. But the witness of a people living in love with one another and living in the love of God comes with authenticity and authority.

The Pentecost church was marked by conformity to Christ's prayer for unity. Acts 1:14 says they were of one accord/purpose/mind (*homothumadon*), devoting themselves to prayer. And it was as they were all together (2:2) and interceding that the Spirit descended upon them at Pentecost. In two subsequent cameos of church life, Luke particularly emphasizes their unity: They devoted themselves to one another (v. 42f.) and were "of one heart and soul" (4:32). The free distribution of goods to those in need demonstrates that this unity was practical, and not just a matter of common intellectual assent to a set of beliefs. Following on from this unity, the next feature of their life together is that everyone was filled with awe (2:43)—always the response to the manifest presence of God.[39] They all experienced great grace upon them (4:33), and knew remarkable effectiveness in witness and conversions to Christ (2:47; 4:33) In Acts we see Jesus' threefold cord in action: unity, leading to anointing, leading to effective gospel witness.

This unity is not conformity—it is a model of relations in the Trinity (John 17:11, 21, 22, 23) where there is distinction without division. Unity is rooted in a shared identity as those who believe and trust in Christ, the Word of God. Unity is grounded in a shared commitment to the apostolic teaching and its witness to salvation through faith in the resurrected Lord Jesus Christ. Unity is fostered by shared prayer together and the sharing of goods with one another.

Unity brings blessing to the believers and is a conduit for God's Word to come with power to unbelievers. Is it worth trying? Is it worth pursuing? Jesus, on the night that He was betrayed, prayed for it. We need to ask ourselves what obstacles in our own personal lives, church life, and denominational life are militating against unity. Then we must repent of our sin, pride, and divisions, and seek in practical ways to restore broken bridges, heal hurts, bandage wounds. Only then will we know what the church in early Acts knew—awe, many miracles, powerful apostolic preaching, great grace upon us all, and the Lord adding daily to our number those being saved.

Step 4—Prayerfulness

Prayer precipitates Pentecost—through the prayers of the Son petitioning the Father (John 14:16) and through the prayers of the church petitioning the Son. The disciples met daily, "devoting themselves in prayer" (Acts 1:14) and preparing themselves for Pentecost, and it was while they were in this togetherness of prayer that the Spirit came upon them (2:2). They knew an ongoing intimacy with God and a manifestation of His power in the context of their corporate prayer (vv. 42f.). In a remarkable passage they experience a second Pentecost: "When they prayed [Greek *deomai*, to beg, beseech], the place in which they were gathered was shaken and they were all filled with the Holy Spirit and spoke the word of God with boldness" (4:31).

Jesus taught us about the equation of prayer and the Spirit: "If you, though you are evil, know how to give good gifts to your children, how much more will your heavenly Father give the Holy Spirit to those who ask" (Luke 11:11f.). Paul understood that prayer and reception of the Spirit are inextricably linked, which is why he was persistent in prayer for the Ephesians and the Colossians that they might receive more of and from the Holy Spirit (Eph. 1:14f.; Col. 1:9f.).

If we are to receive personal Pentecost or an overflowing revival, prayer must be the priority. The saints have always known this. Most know that the Great Awakening in America was fueled by the remarkable sermon from Jonathan Edwards, "Sinners in the Hands of an Angry God." He had preached this sermon several times previously, to no effect. What is little known is that Edwards spent three days and nights in prayer before delivering that sermon again, not eating a morsel, not closing his eyes once, simply petitioning God over and over again: "O Lord, give me New England." God heard, God came, and the rest is history.[40]

Oswald Chambers said that climbing in the Spirit is accomplished by kneeling and not by running.[41] Karl Barth says, "Only where the Spirit is sighed, cried, and prayed for does he become present and newly active."[42] Martyn Lloyd-Jones says, "Plead with him … let him know the despair of your heart. And as soon as you do so, he will grant you your heart's desire. He will speak to you, manifest himself to you, and shed his love abroad in your heart. And you will begin to love him and to rejoice in him and with a joy unspeakable and full of glory."[43]

So let us pray. Let us not rest until we have known that mighty outpouring from on high. Prayer is the key to personal renewal and public revival. Elijah was a man just as we are—he prayed, and heaven gave rain and the earth bore fruit (James 5:17). Oh, how we need the rain of God's Spirit watering the dry and dusty parts of our lives and our land! How we long to be fruit-bearing and not frustrated! If we would know this personal Pentecost, then we must go after it. Here is the Father's promise: "You will seek me and find me when you seek me with all your heart" (Jer. 29:13 NIV). Here is the Savior's promise: "Ask and it shall be given, seek and you will find, knock and the door will be opened to you" (Luke 11:9).

I have an eighty-year-old and very precious booklet on the Welsh Revival that was given to me by my father. Inside is an account by a pastor of how members of his church in 1903 went up every night onto a nearby mountain and prayed for a visitation of God. More and more individuals joined them and soon the Spirit came down on that community, setting God's people ablaze, resulting in many being drawn to Christ. The pastor writes,

> *For fully six months we continued in prayer every night, and the effect of that blessed time is evident even now when the wave of another revival has almost submerged everything. The after effects upon God's people were very great. Speaking for myself, my own heart and life were searched as never before. Was I fully surrendered to the Lord? Where was the power that should be in my ministry? Was I fully assured of salvation? Had I received the Holy Ghost? The outcome of it all was that I yielded wholly to God, casting away all known sin, and making God's glory the one aim of my life and ministry. What an experience followed! What Joy!* [44]

My father, when a young man, wrote on the inside back cover of the booklet, "Prayer, origins of the Revival," and on the inside front cover he wrote, "Oh God, send it now to me."

CHAPTER 6

BAPTIZED WITH OUR BAPTISM

As I noted in the last chapter, the Bible is not systematic in its doctrines and discussion on the person and work of the Spirit. There are several reasons for this.

First, He is God the Lord, perfect in His freedom and aseity. He will not be constrained, confined, or conformed. He is the elusive, powerful river, wind, or fire, flowing, blowing, and glowing where He wills (John 3:8). He will not allow us to put Him in our hermeneutical, theological, or existential boxes.

Second, the Spirit always seeks to push Jesus into center stage, to shine the spotlight on Him. He is not interested in encouraging an interest in Himself, but only in the Son. Indeed, any experience or theology that might lead us to focus our attention and affection on the Spirit is suspect—a very unholy spirit.

Third, the Spirit meets us as individuals, with different psychological, physiological, emotional, and sociological constitutions. The Spirit squeezes into our unique mold in order to mold us in His image. The attempt to manipulate this, to assess other people's experience of God from the basis of our own experience, is often a feature of hegemony, as we want to play God for them, or of our own insecurity, as we want them to conform to our perceived tribal norms. We need to allow God to be God and to blow where and how He wills.

That said, I cannot emphasize enough how Scripture must be the source and norm for all our talk about the Spirit of God and all our testing of what we may think or experience of the Spirit of God. There must be a biblical doctrinal check, and also the check of fruitfulness and faithfulness in Christ, as we walk the long road of obedience in the same direction. But in all our hermeneutic discussion, as we attempt to reconcile the Bible's broad range of theological emphases and experiences with our own, let us hold onto the truth of the Spirit as divine Lord, perfect in His freedom, who blows where He wills, of the primary purpose of the Spirit as promoting Christ, and of the diversity and complexity of us as human beings. Now let us dive into that baptism of the Spirit, always looking to Scripture as our guide.

PENTECOST—BAPTIZED IN THE HOLY SPIRIT

In this chapter I hope to deal with such questions as: What is the baptism of the Holy Spirit? Have I had it? Do I want it? Can I be a Christian and not have it? Am I missing out on something God wants to give me? But first let me clear up the terms we shall use. In the New Testament, baptism is always *in* the Spirit and never *of* the Spirit as the Pentecostals often say. Nor is it a noun, "the baptism of the Spirit," but always a verb, "being baptized in the Spirit."

The correct biblical term, "baptized in the Holy Spirit," is found nowhere in the Old Testament, and only once in each of the Gospels (Matt. 3:11; Mark 1:8; Luke 3:16; John 1:33), twice in Acts (1:5; 11:16), and slightly nuanced by Paul in 1 Corinthians (12:13). Every gospel records it as John the Baptist's promise that after him would come One who would "baptize you in the Holy Spirit." He contrasts his baptism in water with the Messiah's baptism in the Holy Spirit. Mark and John both add a further predicate, "and with fire," to the baptism that Christ brings.

All the gospels omit a definite article with "Holy Spirit," and Mark's economical, pithy Greek also has no prepositions, but uses the dative case, thus literally rendering what he writes, "I baptize you by means of water, but He will baptize you by means of Holy Spirit," where the Holy Spirit is seen as the coagent with Christ of baptism. The Spirit is clearly the element, the "divine milieu," rather than the instrument of the baptism.[1] In Acts 1:5, Jesus takes John's phrase and promises that in just a few days, "you will be baptized in [the] Holy Spirit." When Peter visits and preaches to Cornelius's household, the Spirit of God falls on them and they speak in tongues and prophesy (10:46). In his report back to the apostles in Jerusalem, he says that he recognized in this event their being "baptized with the[2] Holy Spirit" as Jesus had foretold. God was giving these Gentiles the same gift that the Jewish believers had received at Pentecost (11:15f.). Peter's reference to God "baptizing in the Spirit" the Gentiles (v. 17) demonstrates the apostle's understanding that what they experienced at Pentecost (2:1–4) was indeed "baptism in the Spirit." This must also be what was experienced in Samaria (8:14f.) and at Ephesus (19:1f.), in view of the overlapping description of their experiences in all four Pentecosts with the manifestation of "tongues/prophecy" (2:4; 8:18f., seen but not described; 10:46; 19:6) and "the Spirit coming upon/falling upon them" (1:8; 8:16; 10:44; 19:6).

In 1 Corinthians 12:13, Paul says, "For we were all baptized in one Spirit, into one body—whether Jews or Greeks, slave or free—and all were made to drink of one Spirit." We must not miss the context of Paul's argument here as we discuss whether we have or have not received the baptism in the Spirit. Paul is challenging disunity, which has arisen over the claim of some to be more "spiritual" and "gifted" of the Spirit than others. Paul states that the basis of their unity is that they have all been made to drink of one Spirit, they have all been baptized or immersed in the Holy Spirit and united with Christ, thus uniting them in one and the same body, the church (Eph. 1:23; 4:4; 1 Cor. 12:13; Col. 1:18).

Is what Paul describes the same experience, the same baptism, as that prophesied by John, promised by Jesus, and portrayed in Acts? Indeed it is. It follows the response of faith in the gospel proclaimed and manifested (1 Cor. 2:1–5), and it is that divine union with God, by immersion in the Spirit, which also corporately establishes us as the mystical one body of Christ.

Some have claimed that there is a marked difference in terminology here and in action, contending that in the Gospels and Acts there is a baptism by Christ into the Spirit, whereas here in Paul's writing there is a baptism by the Spirit into Christ. Indeed, Lloyd-Jones says that in 1 Corinthians 12 we are seeing something "entirely different" from what is described in the Gospels and Acts in terms of baptism with the Spirit.[3] Even if that view could be proven, it would simply reflect the mutual and reciprocal nature of relations within the Trinity and the interchangeability of divine predicates.[4]

Paul uses an equivalent phrase in 1 Corinthians 12 with the same Greek preposition *en* as in all the other references to baptism in the Holy Spirit (except Mark). Thus 1 Corinthians 12:13 speaks of "baptism in one Spirit" and not "baptism by one Spirit," which, incidentally, we have all experienced. Even the Pentecostal Gordon Fee, in his commentary on Corinthians, counters those charismatics and Pentecostals who wish to interpret this as baptism by/with the Spirit as baptizer, rather than its natural reading as baptism in the Spirit, where the Spirit is the milieu into which the baptized person is immersed. Fee states, "Nowhere else in the New Testament does this dative imply agency, but it always refers to the element 'in which' one is baptized."[5]

David Pawson, by the choice of title for his book *Jesus Baptises in One Holy Spirit*,[6] shows us where he comes down on this question of a distinction in baptisms of the Spirit. Helpfully he shows how, in 1 Corinthians 12:13, "The conjunction of the two prepositions, in and into, governed by the verb 'baptized' … is a parallel and a precedent in John's description of his activity in the Jordan: 'I baptize you in water, into repentance' (Mt. 3:11). 'In' describes the medium in which the person is immersed and 'into' defines the reason or purpose of the immersion."[7]

John's baptism was a baptism in water into repentance; Jesus' baptism is a baptism in the Spirit into the one body of Christ.

It is simply exegetically unacceptable to say that, in the Gospels and Acts, Jesus is the agent and the Holy Spirit the element, while claiming that here in 1 Corinthians 12 it is the Spirit who is the agent and Jesus the element. Paul never says this. Indeed, in Johannine terms, the final clause of verse 13—"all were made to drink of one Spirit"—makes it abundantly plain that it is not the Spirit who is the subject or baptizer, but points instead to Christ, who makes us drink. Unlike the Gospels and Acts citations, Paul does attach to being baptized in the Holy Spirit the further theological adumbration "into one body," but this does not then imply that Paul's baptism here is distinct from the one in the Gospels and Acts. He simply explains some further implications of that selfsame baptism. Paul makes it clear that they have not received, and should not expect to receive, some second and subsequent special endowment of the Spirit as part of the initiation experience, besides union with Christ through baptism in the Spirit.

Let us not miss the whole point of Paul's argument—and his repeated emphasis on the word *all* is to challenge the elitist, charismatic, and rather Gnostic theology, spirituality, and mentality of the Corinthians. This unifying shared experience is further underlined by the threefold repetition in a single verse of the word *one*. Despite different giftings, they must recognize the unanimity of shared experience of the Spirit, having all drunk of the same Spirit, having all been baptized with/in the same Spirit, into Christ, having all believed and responded to the gospel of the crucified Christ that Paul proclaimed.

Within the Pentecostal and charismatic movement, many have used the reference to baptism in 1 Corinthians 12:13 in juxtaposition to the references in the Gospels and Acts to assert that there is both a baptism by the Spirit into Christ (regeneration) and a baptism by Christ into the Spirit (for power). If we add Christ's instruction to be baptized in water (Matt. 28:19), we could actually speak of three separate baptisms. Diagrammatically, it may look like this:[8]

Who is baptized? Baptized into what? Baptized by whom?

- At conversion: the convert into the body of Christ by the Holy Spirit
- At baptism: the Christian in water by the minister
- At Pentecost: the Christian in the Holy Spirit by Jesus Christ

I hope, however, that I have shown that the Spirit baptism of which Paul speaks in 1 Corinthians 12:13 refers to and is synonymous with that Spirit baptism described in the Gospels and Acts and cannot be divorced from regeneration and incorporation into Christ. With this text neutralized for such use, and there being no further scriptural references to baptism in/with the Spirit, the Pentecostal and charismatic claim to dual and distinct baptisms is seriously challenged. For Paul there is baptism in water (1:16f.) and that baptism which all believers are made to drink of, being baptized in the Spirit into Christ, without which we are not Christian, not part of the body. Gordon Fee, in his commentary on 1 Corinthians, says that this is:

> ... *the heart of Pauline theology. What unites the Corinthians is common experience of the Holy Spirit who is manifested in diversity ... For Paul, the reception of the Spirit is the sine qua*

non of the Christian life. The Spirit distinguishes believers from
non (1 Cor. 2:10–14) and above all is what makes a person a
child of God (Rom. 8:14f.).[9]

Thus, a careful study of the grammar, terminology, and theology of all the texts in question indicates that they are all asserting essentially the same thing. Pawson states succinctly that we have the same verb (*baptizein*) with the same preposition (*en*) and the same dative case for Spirit (*Pneumati*).[10] Jesus is the baptizer (agent), the Holy Spirit is the milieu (element) in which the believer is baptized, and every believer, by virtue of his or her faith in Christ, is baptized in the Spirit by Christ. Professor Pickerill helps us here: "The Greek grammar in this statement (1 Cor. 12:13) parallels other passages that speak of being 'baptized in the Holy Spirit'—Mt. 3:11; Mk. 1:8; Lk. 3:16; Jn. 1:33; Acts 1:5; 11:16. While Spirit baptism describes a primary spiritual reality for all believers, Paul still pleads for a Spirit filled experience (Eph. 5:18) which includes the manifestations listed in 1 Cor. 12."[11]

The Pentecostal or charismatic, however, might at this point cry, "Semantics!" It is not an argument over one or two texts they want to win, but a church they want to arm. And they recognize that the church of today often bears little resemblance to the church of the Acts of the Apostles. What seems to be lacking is the presence and power of the Holy Spirit. With Martyn Lloyd-Jones they cry, "Got it all? Well where is it?" If we have what the early church had, they say, why do we not do as the early church did? They have a point. Unless we become seriously dispensational at this point (which would be theologically highly questionable), and claim that the Spirit has changed in His economy and acted then in a way in which He no longer does, then we are forced to face these questions: Why are we not as they were then? Why do we not have what they had then? How are we to get what they had then?

In fact this is part of the thrust of Pawson's book, which exegetically can often be so tight and helpful, but which makes what I consider a serious lapse in judgment when he claims that one can be a Christian, destined to "go to heaven as a forgiven sinner, justified by faith, before receiving the Holy Spirit." Although acknowledging the activity of the Spirit in convicting the sinner and drawing that person to Christ in repentance and faith, Pawson continues:

> *What we must not assume is that this work means either that he has already been "received" or that he already "indwells." Both these terms are kept for Spirit baptism in the New Testament and should be today. Paul's question is still valid: "Having believed, did you receive the Holy Spirit?" (Acts 19:2).*[12]

While I agree with Pawson on the fact of an exact parallel between all references to being baptized in the Spirit in the Gospels, Acts, and 1 Corinthians, I must disagree with him when he claims that one can be a justified believer, post-Pentecost, without being baptized in the Spirit. Paul's very point in 1 Corinthians 12 is that we have all drunk of the one Spirit in whom we were baptized. Paul never envisaged a community in which some were justified and Spirit-baptized and some were just justified. There is not one shred of Pauline teaching to this effect.

We will look in some detail at the Acts 19 text Pawson cites as proof that one can be a Christian without the Spirit, and will show that their reception of the Spirit had not happened because they had not properly believed in Christ and had certainly not received Him—as they had only known John's preparatory baptism and were not yet Christian, hence the need to be instructed, and baptized for repentance and faith in Christ. Not only does the Spirit convict of sin, righteousness, and judgment, leading the sinner to repentance and faith (John 16:8), but He is also the One who regenerates them (3:3–8) and who seals the justified when they hear and believe the gospel (Eph. 1:13). Paul makes it clear that if anyone does not have the Spirit, he or she is not in Christ (Rom. 8:9)—and is presumably not justified either (5:1). Pawson has gone beyond Scripture here, and beyond most Pentecostals and charismatics. I contend that by the Spirit we are convicted and converted. Everyone who repents and turns to Christ has received the Spirit of God indwelling: He or she is born again, regenerated, sealed, a temple of the Spirit, able to bear the fruit of the Spirit. However, there is a level of intimacy with and authority from that indwelling Spirit that many forfeit—there is more of the same—but this is quantitative, not qualitative.

NO MERE SECOND BLESSING

God's Spirit, whom we have miraculously and marvelously received, is not just for our regeneration and sanctification. Through sin, ignorance, apathy, and poor instruction, we can hold back the dam of the Spirit's power within us. Metaphorically speaking, we need to make a breach in the wall, to allow the light to come, the seed to germinate, the clouds to rain, the volcano to erupt, the fuse to reach the dynamite, the giant to awake. Our prayer for being filled with the Spirit is biblical, but one must think in terms of a dinghy containing a compressed air cylinder, simply needing a cord pulled to inflate it. We are to pray for a release from within, and to think of an appropriation, an activation, an actualizing of the Spirit whom we have already received by faith in Christ. There are other external visitations and manifestations from on high, but let's deal with first things first!

We have already noted that Pentecost is the fulfillment and first installment of the promise of being "baptized in the Spirit," and the manifestations there are similarly and subsequently experienced also by the believers at Samaria (Acts 8:14f.), in Cornelius's household (10:44f.), and in Ephesus (19:1f.). This expansion may correspond to Christ's command in Acts 1:8, as the gospel goes out and the church is brought in, from Jerusalem, Judea, Samaria, and the uttermost ends of the earth. Pentecost was Jerusalem, Cornelius was in Judea, the Samaritans were, obviously, in Samaria, and Ephesus represents the uttermost ends of the earth. Nonetheless there are as many vagaries as there are similarities in their initiation into Christ and reception of the Spirit, and any attempt to harmonize them proves futile.

The Pentecostal and indeed the Catholic traditions have made much of a two-stage initiation as seen in Samaria and Ephesus, where reception of the Spirit follows coming to Christ. For the Pentecostals reception of the Spirit is evidenced by tongues and is a subsequent endowment of power, whereas for the Catholics, the emphasis is on the laying on of hands by the apostles and subsequently those bishops in apostolic succession at confirmation, a recognition of full membership of the church and a spiritual strengthening and equipping for service. But serious doubt is cast on whether the so-called disciples in Ephesus (Acts 19:1f.) were Christians before Paul met them and led them to Christ. I believe they were almost certainly not, but were instead followers of John the Baptist, having only received John's anticipatory and preparatory baptism and not having heard about the Holy Spirit, who was such a key feature of the ministry of Christ, even as John preached.[13] Paul needs to instruct them about the Holy Spirit and about Jesus being the One pointed to by John (v. 4), and on hearing this (and presumably accepting it), they must be baptized in the name of Jesus (v. 5) and thus receive the Spirit (v. 6). Unlike the isolated incident at Samaria, Paul is not simply baptizing in the Spirit. Rather he is leading them to Christ, and baptizing them in water, and filling them with the Spirit. Even then, the twofold initiation of baptism and laying on of hands to receive the Spirit is really only one initiation event.

That leaves the story of the church at Samaria (Acts 8:4–25), which is the classic proof text justifying a two-stage initiation in Catholic and Pentecostal thinking. Here there can be no doubt that they were believers, as they had already received the word of the Lord with joy following the preaching of Philip (vv. 4–8, 14). But the Spirit had not yet fallen upon them, despite their correct understanding, belief, and baptism (v. 16). The apostles Peter and John are informed of the Samaritan response to the gospel, and are also perhaps told that they have not received the Spirit (v. 14). They immediately come to Samaria, two days' walk away, and they lay hands on the Samaritans, who immediately receive the Spirit (v. 17) in a visible, tangible manner (v. 18), presumably with tongues and prophecy as with Pentecost, Cornelius, and Ephesus.

If they had believed and been baptized, then the Spirit must already have been active in them convicting of sin and converting to Christ. But there is an apparent manifestation that they lack and that raises alarm bells. There are perhaps three possible reasons for this. First, we have the Pentecostal and Catholic view that they have not received the confirmation/second blessing/baptism in the Spirit. This view is seriously challenged by Paul's teaching that there is only one baptism in the Spirit (1 Cor. 12:13), and they could not have been convicted and converted believers without the Spirit. Second, there is the possibility that they were not really believers (as with the Ephesians) and needed to be initiated properly. This view is ruled out by the fact that, unlike the Ephesians, they are not pointed to Christ or baptized, and they are treated as believers but with a deficient initiation. Third, there is the view that, being the first converts outside Israel, their reception of the Spirit was exceptionally divinely postponed, for pragmatic and prophetic reasons, until the Jewish church leaders had come to legitimatize and authenticate their conversion and had fully accepted them as members of what had now become the international church rather than the internal Jewish sect.[14]

I believe that, in light of the fact that Scripture is clear that no one can become a Christian without the Spirit (John 16:8; Titus 3:5f.; John 3:5f.; Rom. 8:9f.; 1 Peter 1:2; 1 John 3:24), and that there is only one baptism in the Spirit, which is also baptism into Christ and without which we are not in Christ (1 Cor. 12:13), then the third option is the most likely, and we should see the Samaritan believers' undeniable twofold initiation as unique.

Some Catholics and the Pentecostals make the Samaritan story the paradigm for every initiation—i.e., conversion and confirmation/baptism in the Spirit. But far from being the rule, this is shown to be an exception in Acts. If we examine the other conversion or initiation stories in Acts, we surprisingly see no conformity to the pattern in Samaria. We must therefore say that the text in Acts 8 is descriptive of one key specific initiation, but is by no means normative.

A study of every conversion text in Acts is highly instructive here. I have identified twenty-two examples in Acts of individual or group conversions to Christ, post-Pentecost.[15] Of these twenty-two, only one (Samaria, 8:9f.) has a clear-cut, time-lapsed, post-conversion, post-baptism reception of the Spirit. One (Cornelius, 10:44) receives the Spirit and is then immediately baptized. One is baptized then immediately receives the Holy Spirit (Ephesians, Acts 19:1f.). One receives the Spirit and is baptized, but it is unclear in which order (Paul, Acts 9:17f.; compare with 22:12–16). Of the remaining eighteen conversion accounts, five refer to baptism but make no mention of the reception or manifestation of the Spirit, and the remaining thirteen make no reference to either baptism or reception of the Spirit, but simply to belief.

What do we make of this? Samaria is unique. The burden placed on a two-stage initiation by Pentecostals and Catholics is one Luke does not make. Luke's stress is on the belief and reception of the gospel preached by the apostles, which constitutes them as believers. While Luke is silent in most cases about baptism and/or reception of the Spirit, we must surely assume that they were both baptized and received the Spirit according to the command and promise of Christ. But we cannot also assume the timing or mode of reception of the Spirit; we cannot assume that it was either with or without the laying on of hands, with or without speaking in tongues. In three of the twenty-two cases of conversion, reception of the Spirit—as at Pentecost—is manifested with tongues and prophecy. This is shown to be "indicative" of the Spirit's coming, but clearly cannot be proven to be "normative."

Now we may have established as suspect the emphasis placed on certain biblical texts by some Pentecostals and some charismatics and Catholics in order to legitimatize a twofold initiation, but let us not throw the baby out with the bathwater. It strikes me that often what they are doing is attempting to find textual legitimation for what they know to be existentially true. That is, they know they have had an experience of God in terms of power and equipping, often marked with tongues and prophecy. This experience, for many, following months of searching and consecration, has been subsequent to their conversion, often years later, and has been so life-transforming that it appears to them that they never really knew the Spirit before. It has been like a baptism in the Spirit—an immersion, an overwhelming, a drowning in God.

I want to affirm that experience and believe it should be part of the normal Christian life. But I cannot affirm the doctrine. Having believed, they received the Holy Spirit (Eph. 1:13) and were united with Christ in the baptism in the Spirit (1 Cor. 12:13). That Spirit has been at work in them, transforming their characters into the likeness of Christ and using them in service.

It is the Holy Spirit in them who has been driving them to seek more of the Holy Spirit. Hunger for God is an authentic sign of the work of the Spirit.

This newfound experience is marked by immediacy with God—immediacy of God and a deeper revelation of Him, an immediacy in worshipping God, freed to praise Him, and immediacy in communicating with God, as if in an open heaven.[16] Dr. Charles Price, a Presbyterian minister, was suspicious of the Pentecostal claims. He attended a meeting led by the famous Aimee Semple McPherson, intent on pooh-poohing it. But he was moved by the sense of God in that place and the anointing on this woman. At the appeal he went forward and sought the Lord in repentance for renewal. And then the following happened:

> *Something burst within my breast. An ocean of love divine rolled across my heart. This was out of the range of psychology and actions and reactions. This was real. Throwing up both hands I shouted Hallelujah! I ran joyfully through the whole tent, for through the corridors of my mind there marched the heralds of Divine Truth carrying their banners on which I could see emblazoned "Jesus Saves", "Heaven is Real", "Christ Lives Today".[17]*

It strikes me that the charismatic and Pentecostal tradition has the right experience but a flawed doctrine, while the conservative evangelicals have the right doctrine but often a flawed experience. All Christians, by faith in the finished work of Christ, have drunk of that living water and have been baptized in the Spirit, into

Christ. But many have no theology, expectancy, or desire to know the Spirit's power for service, the deep emotional and existential immediacy with God, or the manifestation of the gifts of the Spirit. Those who led us to Christ have not inculcated this expectancy or theology in us. And the Lord who lives with us will not force these things on us. Many are content to live out their Christian lives looking back to the cross and looking forward to heaven without truly tasting now of the age to come by the Holy Spirit (Heb. 6:4f.). The Pentecostals and charismatics may have expressed what they have experienced wrongly, but at least they have experienced it. Many evangelical Christians know biblically that they have been baptized in the Spirit, but do not know it existentially. They are often strangers to the who, what, and why of Him. Their privation is an omission of recognition and appropriation of the Spirit's life. I know I am married to my wife, Tiffany, because of the intimate love we share, not because of the ring or the certificate of marriage. Sadly some Christians know they are baptized in the Spirit by pointing to the document, but have never been on their honeymoon.

BAPTIZED WITH YOUR BAPTISM

In trying to make sense of the relationship between the subjective Pentecostal experience of the Spirit and the objective relationship to the Spirit, Rene Laurentin has helpfully turned to classical Latin theological terms. He refers us to three ancient theological categories: *Sacramentum, Sacramentum et Res,* and *Res.*[18]

First, then, *Sacramentum,* the sign. This is baptism, an external rite that signifies incorporation into Christ. Secondly, we have

Sacramentum et Res, the thing or effect that is also a sign. This is the irreversible mystical incorporation into Christ, through repentance and faith. Thirdly, there is *Res*, the thing itself, the ultimate effect and reality that lies beyond the external rite and the irreversible incorporation. It is the existential knowing of the divine life that is symbolized in *Sacramentum*, and established in *Sacramentum et Res*.

Raniero Cantalamessa says that the grace of the deluging experience of the Holy Spirit spoken of by Pentecostals and charismatics is:

> *a renewal and a reactivation and an actualisation not only of baptism, but of all that Christian initiation represents ... The most common result of this grace is that the Holy Spirit, who before was a more or less abstract object of a person's intellectual assent of faith, becomes a fact of experience.*[19]

This is what David MacInnes terms "being baptised with your baptism," or what the Keswick tradition commonly termed "possessing one's possessions." This is the appropriation of what is already ours in Christ. Laying hold of that which Christ has laid up for us, we enter the Promised Land, which has been given to us.

Influential churchmen like John Stott, Jim Packer, and James Dunn have given us a lead in demonstrating that there are not two baptisms but one—the conversion, regeneration, and initiation experience of the Spirit who baptizes us into Christ. But they have also not been silent in encouraging us to live out the fullness of the life in the Spirit. Sadly, however, many have only looked to such spiritual masters for their biblical exposition, and have not followed that through into the life in the Spirit to which they exhort us.

John Stott encourages us to grow in the power of the Spirit toward maturity, knowing "a deeper, fuller, richer experience of God."[20] Jim Packer reproves us thus: "Today's biblical Christians, wherever else they are strong, are weak on the inner life—and it shows." He affirms the experiences and witnesses of the Spirit that "intensify a quality of experience, that is real in some measure for every believer from the first."[21] The notable antagonist against a Pentecostal doctrine, Leonard Steiner, has declared, "There are numerous genuine examples of the [Pentecostal] experience of the Spirit without there being a correct understanding of the Spirit."[22] James Dunn, having deconstructed Pentecostalist two-stage initiation theology, declares,

> *The positive value of the Pentecostal emphasis is his highlighting of the dramatic nature of the initiating Spirit baptism; the Spirit not only renews, he equips for service and witness. Yet however correct Pentecostals are to point to a fresh empowering of the Spirit as the answer to the Church's sickness they are quite wrong to call it "the baptism in the Spirit". One does not enter the new age or the Christian life more than once, but one may be empowered by or filled with the Spirit many times.*[23]

Harold Hoehner, in his exhaustive treatment of Ephesians, has made an acute observation contrasting Paul's clear instruction to be Spirit filled with the total absence of any similar imperative to be baptized in the Spirit:

It is interesting to note that the indwelling, sealing and baptizing ministries of the Spirit are bestowed on every believer at the time of salvation. There are no injunctions for the believer regarding them because they are an integral part of the gift of salvation. For example, if you are not indwelt by the Holy Spirit, then you are not a believer (Rom. 8:9). On the other hand, "be filled by" and "walk by" the Spirit expressed in the present imperative[24] indicates that this is not an automatic bestowment at the time of salvation but an injunction for every believer to follow continually.[25]

FILLED WITH THE FULLNESS

"One baptism, many fillings" may sound like something of a cliché, but it is the weight of the New Testament on this issue. Almost a century ago, W. H. Griffiths-Thomas, the principal of Wycliffe Hall, Oxford, wrote,

While believing that a Spirit filled life is the privilege and duty of every believer, and that as a matter of personal experience it is often realised by means of a distinct crisis after conversion, yet much modern phraseology about "the baptism of the Spirit" does not seem to be justified by the New Testament which teaches that all who are born again have been baptised into one body of Christ.[26]

When all is said and done concerning being baptized in the Spirit, the fact that in Acts we see the same people filled with the Spirit successively and manifestly (Acts 2:1–4; 4:8, 31; 13:9), and the fact that we see Paul's prayers in Ephesians 1 and 3 and Colossians 1 for the Christians to know a deeper, richer, fuller experience by the Spirit, all rather takes the steam out of those who point to having "got it all," whether conservatives at conversion, Pentecostals at second blessing, or Catholics at confirmation. Paul writes the most comprehensive statement on salvation to the Romans, but adds that he longs to visit them in order to impart apostolically an apparently absent, but presumably significant, gifting of the Spirit (Rom. 1:11; 15:29). Paul acknowledges that the Corinthians have received spiritual gifts (1 Cor. 12), and despite the fact that they have misused them and are lacking in Christian character, he still encourages them to eagerly desire more of the greater gifts of the Spirit (12:31; 14:1). The Galatian Christians are reminded that they have received the Spirit (Gal. 3:2), but they must now keep in step with the Spirit (5:16–25). Paul says the Ephesian Christians possess the Spirit (Eph. 1:14), but he does not leave it there. He prays that they may receive a greater strengthening and knowledge of God's love by the Spirit (3:16f.), exhorts them not to grieve the Spirit (4:30), and commands that they be continually filled with the Spirit (5:18). Paul makes it abundantly clear: There is abundantly more!

Throughout this book I have given illustrations and quotations from those who have found "more"—a deeper, fuller, richer, more powerful, more joyful, more fruitful life in the Spirit, often precipitated by a dramatic experience or deep revelation. Some, like the Pentecostals, call this "the seal or baptism of the Spirit"; charismatics call it "the second blessing," "the Spirit-filled life," or "Spirit fullness";

others from the Keswick tradition speak of it in terms of the "higher life," or "victorious Christian living," or the "abiding life," and those in the holiness tradition speak (wrongly) of the experience in terms of "perfection."

I already stated in chapter 1 that I prefer to use the phrase "filled with the fullness." How what is ours in Christ (Col. 2:10) becomes ours in experience (Eph. 3:19) is stated succinctly by O'Brien:

> *They are to become what they already are ... and being filled by the Spirit is an important means in the process. When the apostle desires that his readers may be strengthened through the Spirit and experience the effects of Christ indwelling so that they may be "filled with all the fullness of God", he is praying that they may be all that God wants them to be.*[27]

Something that they clearly are not! Andrew Lincoln says,

> *The fullness of God, which is best explained as his presence and power, his life and rule, immanent in his creation, has been mediated to believers through Christ (Col. 1:29—2:10), in whom the fullness was present bodily ... It is expressed in the passive and absolute form. Presumably this is a divine passive—they are to be filled by God—and presumably if they are to be filled up to the fullness of God, it is with this fullness that they are to be filled ... As believers are strengthened through the Spirit in the inner person, as they allow Christ to dwell in their hearts through faith, and as they know more of the love of Christ, so the process of being filled up to all the*

fullness of the life and power of God will take place. Response to
the imperative of Eph. 5:18 "be filled with the Spirit" will also
be part of the realization of this process.[28]

Paul's choice of verbs, "going on being filled with the Spirit,"
suggests, as the charismatic leader Jack Hayford has noted, that,
"All the fullness of God speaks of more than one experience or one
aspect of his truth or power. It points to a broad spirituality bal-
anced through participating in all God's blessings, resources and
wisdom."[29] This fullness does not come through a one-off experience
of God, but through an ongoing entering into all He has given to
us in Christ. It comes through the disciplines of prayer, study, worship, giving, consecration, holiness, and witness. It comes through
ministry and the laying on of hands. It comes through a life lived
in obedience. It comes through self-denial and death to the flesh. It
comes through the revelation by the Spirit and the Word of God.
It is a movement into a life that is ours through the cross and the
Spirit. Baptism in the Spirit into Christ is only the beginning. There
is much more to come!

CHAPTER 7

RESURRECTION POWER, FELLOWSHIP SUFFERINGS

Recently my son Joel returned from children's church with his craftwork. The class had been learning about Pentecost and had cut out and colored four-inch cardboard flames to symbolize the coming and empowering of the Spirit. For once I was thrilled to see that Joel had decided to do his own thing. He had stapled together two straws to make a cross and had then attached the cardboard flames to the top of the cross. Joel told me he had wanted to be creative; in fact he was reflecting something deeply profound and theologically vital.

THE PLACE OF THE SKULL

Luther taught us that we must not substitute a *theologia gloria* (a theology centered on glory) for the primacy of the *theologia crucis* (a theology centered on the cross). In fact it is not an either/or but an indivisible both/and—the Spirit of glory leads us to the cross from which is released the Spirit of glory. If, as John's gospel hints, the cross was part of Christ's glory, not just a pathway to it, and if we desire the glory of God in our life, then we must go to Calvary and learn with Paul that we glory in the cross (Gal. 6:14).

The glory of the Spirit-filled life flows from the agony of the cross-shaped life. Only as we constantly identify with the cross of Christ can we expect to know the power of the Spirit that gushes from it. The river of life flows from the place of the skull. The tired, dry, weary, worn-down believer whose pilgrimage has substituted drudgery for delight must constantly come to the river of life at the place of the skull. The struggling, compromised, backsliding believer must come back to the river of life at the place of the skull. The desperate believer longing for a greater anointing to serve Christ more effectively must come to the river of life at the place of the skull. The maturing believer who is longing for a greater, deeper intimacy with the Savior must come to the river of life at the place of the skull.

At the cross Jesus not only wonderfully took the punishment for our sin and purchased our salvation, but He released that river of living water so that we would never thirst again. There flowed from His side a river of blood and water (John 19:34), which was not merely a scientific proof of death,[1] but a symbolic pointer to Christ's death as the opening to life in the Spirit. Those two streams keep flowing together—blood and water, Calvary and Pentecost, salvation and satisfaction.

Those two rivers[2] never run dry, but we can fail to run into them and we can stay dry. We must constantly come to the cross, both for cleansing of sin by that river of blood and for renewing by the

Spirit in that river of water. Sadly some within the church have made a dichotomy, divorcing the two streams, wanting Calvary without Pentecost or Pentecost without Calvary. Some charismatics try to run before they can walk, and perhaps some conservatives are walking but do not realize that they are also made to run.

The early church understood the need to see these key elements held together. Lampe, in his work on confirmation, showed that from the very earliest times, reception of converts to Christ was accompanied by baptism in water (signifying death and life with Christ), anointing with oil (representing the Holy Spirit), and signing with the cross. Only subsequently—and pastorally disastrously—did these get divided up liturgically.[3]

Some Christian movements have sought to restore this understanding. Round my neck I always wear the powerful symbol of the sixteenth-century French Calvinist Huguenots—a cross with a dove descending from it. The Salvation Army has as its motto and banner "Blood and Fire." Following the outpouring of the Spirit at Azusa Street and the birth of the Pentecostal movement, its leaders produced a statement titled "The Apostolic Faith" to present its core doctrinal understandings. In discussing the relationship of this newfound experience of the Spirit with the cross, they wrote:

> *The Holy Ghost never died for our sins. It was Jesus who died for our sins and it is his blood that atones for our sins ... 1 Jn 1:9, 7 ... It is the blood that cleanses and makes holy, and through the blood we receive the baptism of the Holy Spirit. The Holy Ghost falls in answer to the blood.*[4]

Tom Smail, a leading exponent of charismatic renewal in the 1970s, wrote of the remarkable, and very insightful, experience of the first time he gave a prophetic word in tongues at a charismatic meeting. A young woman gave the interpretation: "There is no way to Pentecost except by Calvary; the Spirit is given from the cross."[5] This revelation was one that made a deep impact on the young theologian Smail, and it anchored his theology and armed his ministry as teacher to the flourishing charismatic movement in those heady days of new wine.

There is a deep current through John's gospel that intertwines the themes of our salvation and satisfaction with the Spirit's impartation through Christ's crucifixion and glorification. In John 4, Jesus speaks to the woman at the well and promises that if she believes in Him, He will give her to drink of the living water and she will "never thirst again" and will "receive eternal life" (John 4:14)—i.e., existential satisfaction and eternal salvation. In John 7:37f., Jesus repeats this invitation to drink from Him of the living water, "by which He meant the Holy Spirit, who had not yet been given because Jesus was not yet glorified." In John 16, Jesus speaks of His departure and our investiture of the Spirit, who flows from the cross but directs us to the cross, convicting us of sin, righteousness, and judgment (vv. 8–11), directing us to a greater truth of Christ (v. 13) and seeking to glorify Christ by taking what is His and revealing it to us (v. 14). As His arrest and crucifixion draw near, Jesus prays (17:1) that He might be glorified through His bestowing of eternal life, soon to be activated at the cross. Jesus' last words from the cross are "I thirst," and then, we are told, "He gave up His spirit" (19:28–30). Is John hinting here not just at Christ's release from life, but His release of the Spirit? In fact, in the Greek it does not have a personal pronoun but a definite article: not "gave up His spirit," but "gave up the spirit." Larry Kreitzer says that John here intends a "deliberate piece of double meaning. Who within the Johannine community could have ever read or heard this and not recognized that it is deliberately intended to involve thoughts of the Paraclete?"[6]

While the Spirit would not actually be given by Christ until His ascension, in John's theology the cross is the place where that gift is secured and sent. Jesus thirsted so that we do not have to. The promise of our satisfaction by the Spirit is found on a trajectory from Christ's crucifixion. He gave up His spirit so that we might receive His Spirit. His glory is His agony for our glory. Let us come to the river of life at the place of the skull.

This wedding of the Spirit to the cross is a theme anticipated and demonstrated throughout Scripture. In Exodus 29:21 we see the appointing of Aaron to high-priestly office. He is sprinkled both by the blood of the ram and by the anointing oil. The blood covers his sin; the oil—symbolic of the Spirit's anointing (1 Sam. 16:13)—sets him apart and equips him for ministry.

At Jesus' baptism we see Him going into the water as a full identification with God's call through John to repent—a full identification with sinful humankind, who are called to repent and prepare for the coming kingdom. There the Holy Spirit falls upon Him as God fully identifies with Jesus in this act: "This is My beloved Son" (Luke 3:22). This baptism is prophetic identification but also prophetic anticipation. Jesus' immersion in water is a prophetic foreshadowing of His immersion in His own blood at Calvary.

Jesus said to His disciples, "Can you drink the cup I must drink, or be baptized with the baptism with which I must be baptized?" (Mark 10:38). This baptism, pointing to His cross, is also the place where Jesus receives the Holy Spirit (Luke 3:22; 4:1). John the Baptist declared that Jesus was "the Lamb of God who takes away the sin of the world" (John 1:29), and following His baptism in which the Spirit descended on Him as a dove, declared Him to be "the baptizer with the Holy Spirit" (v. 1:33). Thus it is at the cross that Christ secures the release of the Spirit for us. The Lamb and the dove, the blood and the Spirit, walk hand in hand.

In Acts we read how the Holy Spirit came at Pentecost and filled the waiting, praying, faithful few in the upper room (Acts 1:13; 2:3). The "upper room" is pregnant symbolically as the place where Christ reenacted the Passover supper, pointing to His imminent fulfillment of all that the rite symbolized at Calvary, where His body and His blood would be given for them (Luke 22:1–20, esp. v. 12). Luke's reference (Acts 1:13) to the disciples, post-ascension, meeting, praying, and waiting in the "upper room" for the gift of the Holy Spirit, and the coming of the Spirit upon them in that very room (2:1f.),[7] is more than a literary link—it is a prophetic correspondence. The place where they heard and saw Christ speak of the new covenant established in His blood is the place where the Spirit comes to inaugurate the new covenant.

Filled with the Spirit, they spilled out onto the streets and declared the wonders of God. What were these wonders? They can surely be none other than Jesus Christ, crucified, risen, glorified, confirmed by the sending of the Spirit. The Spirit-filled Peter stands in the midst of the bemused crowd and preaches—not his or their experience per se, but his Savior's cross and the gift of salvation in and through that name. The startled hearers may receive the same Holy Spirit if they repent and are baptized in the name of Jesus, identifying fully with His death and resurrection (Acts 2:38). Later, when Peter visits Cornelius, Scripture makes it very plain that it is as he is speaking words about the cross and resurrection of Christ that the Holy Spirit falls on those listening (10:38f., 44).

Writing to the somewhat chaotic and compromised church of Corinth, Paul seeks to ground their eccentric and elitist charismatic spirituality by anchoring it firmly in the cross. In his first letter to the Corinthians, Paul reminds them that the initial evidences and encounter with the Spirit (1 Cor. 2:4) came through his own weak and foolish preaching (v. 3) concerning the apparently weak and foolish scarred God of Calvary (1:23). Paul is challenging them on many fronts in this letter, but not least on the fact that they have moved on to higher things in the name of the *pneuma*, but have in fact left the true Spirit behind.

This same point is being made in Paul's letter to the Galatians, although the manifestation of their error is the opposite of the Corinthians—not license but legalism. Only the Holy Spirit can walk us between these two errors, "Holy" as a balance to license, "Spirit" implying a balance to law (2 Cor. 3:6). In Galatians 3:1f., Paul rebukes the church for deviating from Christ Jesus, who was presented before them as crucified—thus satisfying the demands of the law—and it was through faith in this crucified Christ that they received the Spirit (v. 2), presumably an event Paul is able to point to as tangible and memorable.

In the earliest of Eucharistic liturgies dating from the third and fourth centuries, prayers known as the *epiclesis* (Greek for "calling down/upon") were made to the Holy Spirit to visit the symbols of bread and wine in order to enable them to be to us the body and blood of our Savior. The early Fathers understood that the Spirit led us to the cross and the cross to us. The Spirit is always found and grounded in the cross. We grieve the Spirit when we leave the cross behind, and we receive the Spirit when the cross takes center stage.

BACK TO THE CROSS

The Spirit-filled Christian will constantly be drawn to the cross. The person who lives and loves the cross will constantly be drawn to a deeper understanding and experience of the Spirit. There is a mutual, reciprocal, and indivisible relationship between the cross and Spirit. This is the Christian criterion for our theology, our ministry, and our spirituality; this is the Christian cycle—being led from the cross to a deeper life in the Spirit, which leads us back to a deeper identification with Christ at the cross.

Jesus says He is looking for those who worship in Spirit and truth (John 4:23f.). Paul tells us that "we are the true circumcision who worship in the Spirit of God and glory in Christ Jesus and put no confidence in the flesh" (Phil. 3:3). That truthful, Spirit-filled worship will always point to Calvary.

In the subsequent life of the church, it is interesting to observe how those movements of the visitation of the Holy Spirit inevitably restore a deeper understanding and intimacy with the cross. I believe that one of the core fruits and tests of a genuine work of the Spirit is a greater passion for mission and for Christ-centered, cross-centered worship. The remarkable Moravian renewal of life in the Spirit saw both a passion for worldwide evangelistic mission and a placing of the Lord's Supper at the center of their life together. The Great Awakening, with its radical evangelization campaigns, stemmed from personal renewal of the Holy Spirit in such men as the Wesley brothers and George Whitefield. Here again the personal experience of the Spirit brought witness to the cross. The sermons on salvation were echoed in Charles Wesley's songs: "And can it be that I should gain an interest in the Savior's blood?" While songs of intimacy, desire, and personal expression of devotion to Christ always feature in a movement of spiritual renewal, another constant is always the re-presentation and re-appreciation of the cross.

The Pentecostal revival of the early twentieth century saw a resurgence of worship choruses that asked, "What can wash you white as snow? Nothing but the blood of Jesus," and declared, "There is power, power, wonder-working power in the precious blood of the Lamb." The charismatic renewal of the 1980s saw Graham Kendrick writing classics such as "The Price Is Paid" and "Led like a Lamb." The move of the Spirit amongst the youth generation in the 1990s resulted in new worship leaders like Matt Redman writing such outstanding songs as "I Will Love You for the Cross," "Thank You for the Blood," and the beautiful "You Led Me to the Cross" with its timeless line, "Now that I'm living in Your all-forgiving love, my every road leads to the cross."[8] These hymn writers, and one could name many more besides, are not trained academic theologians who have spent years analyzing the biblical metaphors of the atonement. They are disciples who have been personally impacted by a deep renewal of the Holy Spirit and drawn back to the cross, seeking to articulate this experience in song and inviting us to join them at the cross.

I recently heard a testimony from a student at Oxford who told of how she had come to Christ for salvation but resisted the more dramatic experiences she was witnessing as the Spirit moved upon others. She was afraid that the Spirit (or something else) would make her act in a foolish manner, and in particular she feared falling over in public, which she thought utterly unnecessary and unseemly. After many weeks, she went forward for prayer, all the while resisting any idea that the Holy Spirit might visit her with a visible manifestation of His presence. The Lord clearly thought differently, and when the Spirit fell upon her, she fell to the ground and lay there in the healing embrace of Christ. When she subsequently told of her experience, she joyfully and boldly described how, as the Spirit made her lie down in green pastures, restoring her soul, she was given a vision of the cross of Christ and the love of God. I questioned her about this encounter, and she reiterated that it was the deeper revelation through the vision of Calvary that had reassured her that this was indeed the Holy Spirit. The Holy Spirit who flows from the cross will always lead us to the cross.

COME DIE WITH ME

Teresa of Avila said, "I saw myself dying with a desire to see God and I knew not how to seek that life otherwise than by dying."[9]

As we have said, those who wish to be in the flow of the Spirit will inevitably be drawn back to the cross. This is not merely for appreciation through a greater revelation of Christ's atoning substitutionary sacrifice, but for a deeper identification with and incorporation into the crucified life. Spiritual men and women who desire more of God will constantly learn the painful lesson of personal crucifixion. Only as we die do we live, only as we lay down our lives are they resurrected in the power of the Spirit, only as we hide ourselves in the wounds of Christ is the ongoing healing, saving power of the cross manifested through us. Salvation—our eternal destiny—is never in doubt. By faith in Christ as Lord and Savior and by repentance of sins we secure this once for all. But there is a temporal appropriation many miss out on because they fail to carry their cross daily.

We must not lose sight of the fact that the Spirit fell on Jesus as He was buried in the waters of baptism—that prophetic place of death (Matt. 4:16). That same dove rests on us as we constantly go down into our baptism waters of death. In the Catholic tradition, at the entrance to the church, there is usually a small well, called a stoup, containing water from previous baptisms. As people enter the church, they dip a finger in the water and sign their forehead with the cross. This is a powerful reminder that they may only enter that place set apart for meeting God through a personal appropriation of their baptism, which signifies their deathly union with Christ at Calvary.

While we may not wish to sign ourselves constantly with the cross in baptism water, by the Spirit, God will constantly be leading us to reaffirm and reappropriate our baptism in water, speaking of our baptism into Christ. And as William Willimon rightly says, "The chief biblical analogy for baptism is not the water that washes but the flood that drowns."[10]

MY DARK NIGHT OF THE SOUL

When I went to theological college to start my training for the ordained ministry, I was on a personal and spiritual high. I had just come from several years of successful pastoral ministry in church-planting, in which we saw a handful of people become a strong and vibrant new church. I felt secure in my ministry, identity, and destiny—I was loved and accepted by my church community, and I knew the hand of the Lord was upon me, clearly leading me to the Anglican ordained ministry. On the first day at college, a fellow student whom I already knew and respected told me that he felt he had a word for me from John 12:24: "I tell you the truth, unless a kernel of wheat falls to the ground and dies, it remains only a single seed. But if it dies, it produces many seeds" (NIV). Here Jesus was speaking prophetically about His own imminent death, which would bear great fruit, but it seemed God was saying that my time at college would be my own place of death and burial. I was not sure what to make of it—but I was soon to learn what Bonhoeffer meant when he said, "When Jesus calls a man, he bids him come and die."[11]

I soon realized how much my identity and security derived from what I did for Christ rather than from who I am in Christ. I was Simon, the preacher, evangelist, mentor, minister, ghost-buster, all-around good egg, and still only twenty-five years old! But when the ministry was taken away, when there was no longer a sermon to preach or someone to pastor, when there was just me in a classroom of thirty others who had the same gifts or greater, when I was just one among many—a nameless, faceless, powerless student at a desk struggling with Greek verbs—the shallow veneer of my spirituality began to crack, and up from within rose the old man, whom I thought I had left at Calvary, but who returned like a zombie to haunt me. As the weeks and months went by, although I was succeeding academically, I was having a breakdown on the inside.

I was being slowly stripped to the core, and a mirror was held up to my own sinful, compromised, pride-filled, corrupt self. Dark and demonic thoughts crowded into my mind—it seemed as if every evil spirit I had ever disturbed, challenged, or evicted had come to pay me a visit with their family. Ministry, prayer, fasting, standing by faith, and spiritual disciplines all seemed futile against this torrent of darkness.

I had always been so confident in public speaking, but now I broke into a sweat at the thought of doing a reading in chapel. I had always loved being with people, the center of the crowd, but now all I wanted to do was to hide away. I had always felt I was a first-class role model for Christian leadership, but now I saw that I was largely a fraud with a deep and murky cesspit of sin and self in my inner man. I thought I ought to pull back from ministry, but a few faithful and wise Christians prayed with me, counseled me, and carried me through that dark night of the soul.

The last words of the film *Apocalypse Now*, based on Joseph Conrad's book *Heart of Darkness*, are the haunting, "The horror, the horror." I believe the Lord Jesus allowed me—a born-again,

Spirit-filled minister of the gospel—to visit the place of horror that is humanity's condition without God's grace. He was saying to me, "This is what you are without Me!" Besides learning about myself through this stripping, breaking, and deep reordering of my soul, I also learned with the psalmist that "Though I make my home in Sheol, God is there" (Ps. 139:8). Even in the darkest night God set stars to guide me. I was hanging on to my mind and my faith by my fingertips, but God's strong hand was not going to let me go. Slowly God began to bring me out of this miry pit and place my feet upon a rock. Slowly this grain of my life that had been buried and cracked open was beginning to rise to life again. Only time will tell if there are many seeds produced, but in the ten or so years since that bleak and black time, I and others can testify to a greater anointing, greater dependence, greater desire for intimacy, and a wider influence than I might ever have expected beforehand. God be praised!

While I was writing this book, a member of my church with a strong prophetic gift came to church one Sunday and handed me a pomegranate. This person did not know that "Pomegranate" had been a nickname of mine at school. She simply said that she sensed the Lord was saying that even as the pomegranate has many seeds, so the Lord had placed many seeds within me to bear fruit for His kingdom. May it be that the seed that died is resurrected thirty, sixty, one hundredfold.

John the Baptist made the remarkable selfless statement, "He must increase, I must decrease" (John 3:30). He understood that he existed simply to make way for Jesus, to get out of the way of Jesus. The same is true for us. If we truly desire to see Christ glorified in and through us, then He must be seen and we must get out of the way. The sincere prayer for more is the prayer, "Lord, You must increase, I must decrease"—and that is a prayer that costs us dearly.

I discovered firsthand that the Christian life is the way of the cross, a path of both glory and agony. God does not want to patch up the old me; He wants to kill that old man and raise me to new life with His life living through me. I understood, with Kierkegaard, that "God creates everything out of nothing (ex nihilo)—and everything which God is to use he first reduces to nothing."[12] God does not want a beautiful alabaster vase set aside to be admired, but a broken one with its contents poured out in worship (Mark 14:1f.). God wants a clay vessel, so that His glory within may shine out (2 Cor. 4:7). The way of the Spirit is the way of the cross. Being filled with the Spirit means being emptied. Tom Smail writes, "A spirit who could derogate from the glory of Christ crucified in order to promote a more dazzling glory of his own, who passes by the sufferings of Christ in order to offer us a share in a painless and costless triumph, is certainly not the Holy Spirit of the New Testament."[13]

BROKEN

The story of the great East African revival between the 1930s and 1960s is recorded in the tellingly titled *The Calvary Road*[14] by Roy Hession, a minister much used by God to fuel the flames of church renewal and social revival.[15] The basic thesis is that personal and national revival are the result of a deep work of the Spirit emanating from "brokenness" before the cross. Hession says that revival may be "as wide as the response to the call to brokenness at the cross."[16]

Brokenness is the key concept to personal revival spilling over to impact society. A deep humility before the crucified Lamb opens the floodgates of heaven's blessing. It is helpful to quote this godly gospel minister at length:

> *... the outward forms of such revivals do of course differ considerably, but the inward and permanent content of them all is always the same—a new experience of conviction of sin among the saints; a new vision of the cross of Jesus and of redemption; a new willingness on man's part for brokenness, repentance, confession and restitution; a joyful experience of the power of the blood of Jesus to cleanse fully from sin and restore and heal all that sin has lost and broken; a new entering into the fullness of the Holy Spirit and of His power to do His own work through His people, and a new gathering in of the lost ones to Jesus.*[17]

This was not an academic understanding, but birthed out of Hession's own personal wrestling with God in a place of barrenness and brokenness, in which he felt his evangelistic ministry had lost the power of the Holy Spirit. Following a message and testimony by some African brothers at an Easter conference in 1947, Hession watched his wife and colleagues grasp that being filled with the Spirit comes through being broken at the cross and come into that place of purity and power. Finally, unable to watch from the sidelines any longer, Hession sought the Lord, confessing again his sins, knowing again the cleansing of the blood and the new anointing of God's Spirit. The lesson was clear: Spiritual barrenness must lead us to brokenness at the cross, from which flows forgiveness and fruitfulness.

There must be a fellowship with Christ's sufferings if there is to be a true knowing of Christ and a sharing in the power of the resurrection (Phil. 3:10). But how hard the flesh resists such mortification! How much the church has bought into the self-help, materialistic, narcissistic, hedonistic values of this world!

Mark Stibbe has written helpfully on brokenness, death, and self-emptying as an essential ingredient in revivals, and he cites the experiences of Wesley in the Great Awakening, Douglas Brown in the Lowestoft revival, and Duncan Campbell in the Hebridean revival.[18] In private correspondence with me, Stibbe wrote:

> *I think the key to receiving more [seen] in revival and scripture is the death process. This is where the cross and the Spirit relate. My reading of both Bible and history would indicate that fresh outpourings of the Spirit often come to a person or a group of people who come to a new place of surrender to God. Revival is more of the Spirit, but it comes via more of the cross! When it comes the Spirit leads to the cross even as … the cross leads to the Spirit.*

GOD WANTS US DEAD NOT ALIVE

In the 1960s Bond movie *Goldfinger*, James Bond is lying strapped to a table with a laser beam about to cut him in half. Bond asks

Goldfinger, "Do you expect me to talk?" Goldfinger replies, "No, Mr. Bond, I expect you to die."

In Romans 6, Paul speaks of the spiritual death of the believer. It is significant that this chapter follows on from his discussion on justification by faith (chapter 5) and precedes the chapters on union with Christ (chapter 7) and life in the Spirit (chapter 8). While we must resist seeing these as four distinct movements or moments in the Christian's life, all of them taking place in actuality through Christ and in the believer at conversion, the logical flow of Paul's argument suggests that these features of the Christian life must be personally actualized.

Union with Christ, achieving our salvation, is symbolized by baptism—and this imagery is not primarily about washing but about dying. Paul writes,

> *Do you not know that all of us who were baptized into Christ Jesus were baptized into His death? We were buried with Him through baptism into His death, so that just as Christ was raised from the dead through the Father's glory, we too might walk in newness of life … Our old self was crucified with Him in order that our body of sin might be done away with. (Rom. 6:3–6)*

Elsewhere Paul describes it thus: "I have been crucified with Christ and I no longer live, but Christ lives in me" (Gal. 2:20 NIV). The problem is that many of us fail to live the new life of the united believer joined to Christ, but instead still live the old life of our sinful, Adamic flesh. Our Christian life is often like a horror story in which the dead return to hound, haunt, and hinder the living. The old man is dead, but not buried.

Thus Paul can command, "Consider yourselves dead to sin but alive to Christ!" (Rom. 6:11). The imperative "consider" (Greek *logisesthai*) implies a mental, logical, calculating reasoning that effects action, whereby we remind ourselves that we are dead men walking, and refuse to be haunted by our own old ghost but make ourselves home to the Holy Ghost. The problem is, we constantly want to resurrect the dead in our own lives, and consequently disobey God by communicating with the departed. We fail to see that we are dead men and that we live only by, in, and for Jesus.

The conservative exegete Professor Gerald Hawthorne gets to the heart of the matter, explaining Paul's desire to know fully whom he has believed:

> *Paul desired to come to know Christ more fully, not as a theological topic to be discussed, much as he had used to discuss different points of the Jewish Law, but as a person to be enjoyed. He desired to experience in practice what he knew to be true in theory; i.e. that when Christ died he [Paul] died; when Christ was resurrected he too was resurrected. He desired to sense within himself the power of the resurrected living Christ. He desired to realize in personal experience the fact that Christ's suffering for sin had indeed put to the death his sin. To this end Paul, although indeed dead to sin by virtue of Christ's death for him, nevertheless, by his own continuous, conscious choice was prepared to take this fact seriously, to take sides with Christ against himself,*

to bring his practice in the world in line with his position in Christ.[19]

All That You Can't Leave Behind is an album title by the rock band U2. We cannot live the new life of union with Christ in the Spirit until we leave the old life behind. Jesus said, "If anyone would come after Me, they must deny themselves, take up their cross and follow Me" (Matt. 16:24)—only we so often would rather try and come after Him carrying our baggage and not the cross. We want to have our cake and eat it—we want Christ, the new life, the new man, and a piece of the old. We resist the cross: It is a killer, it is not for makeovers, no one ever recovered from crucifixion, it kills all known sins dead. A. W. Tozer said, "The man on the cross is facing only one direction; he's not going back; he has no further plans of his own." But our mortal coil recoils from this mortification of the flesh. We want a spiritual botox injection, not decapitation. And so, unlike Paul, who declared, "I die daily" (1 Cor. 15:31), daily choosing to resist the flesh, to keep the old man in his coffin, and to follow a new life as the new man in Christ, we would rather climb off the uncomfortable cross, get out of the baptistery for fear of drowning, and jump off the altar for fear of being consumed.

I love the story of C. T. Studd, the Eton and Cambridge scholar who, as England's cricket captain, had been destined for worldly fame and fortune. He forsook it all to make Christ known as a pioneer missionary in China and then the Congo, and in so doing won honors in the church's hall of fame and an eternal fortune. On one occasion he led a campaign that caused offense to many but underlined the idea of being dead to everything but Christ. He called it the "DCD Campaign," and the initials stood for "Don't Care a Damn." He designed a logo with this DCD monograph, incorporating a skull and crossbones, and placed this on his literature, headed paper, jackets, stickers, and so on. His point was that for him to live was Christ, and he did not care about anything else. He was dead to everything but Christ.[20]

George Müller, that remarkable minister to the poor and orphaned in Bristol, was once asked the secret of his success. He replied, "There was a day when I died: died to George Müller, his opinions, preferences, tastes and will; died to the world, its approval or censure; died to the approval or blame even of my brethren and friends, and since then I have studied only to show myself approved unto God." Dead men have no ambitions, affections, volitions, opinions. The dead have no interest in fashion or in their future, and they have no fear. Dead men tell no tales, neither do they sin. "Anyone who has died has been freed from sin" (Rom. 6:7 NIV). This speaks not only of the penalty of sin, not only of the power of sin, but surely also of the presence of sin. God needs to remove that rotting flesh to make way for the new life. He needs to get us out of the picture, so that He might put Christ there. As we come to the cross, as we submit to His will, as we repent and renounce sin, as we die another day, as we receive the Holy Spirit, as we choose to walk in the Spirit, so we become who we are, and the life and glory of God are manifested through us.

Billy Graham was once asked how he managed to resist the temptations of attraction to the opposite sex. He replied, "I am dead to every woman but my wife Ruth." Was he? Did he not find other women attractive? Of course he did. But he chose to say no. He understood the position (Rom. 6:8–10): He had died with Christ and to sin. He understood the psychology (v. 11): He considered himself dead to sin. He understood the practice (v. 12): He was not to let sin reign in his mortal body to the extent that he obeyed its lusts.

That old Adamic fallen sinful nature—*sarx*, or flesh—is the cause of our sin, and the cause of our grieving the Holy Spirit. We need to remind this old man that he is dead and must stay buried. We were buried with Christ at baptism. We are not to be rebaptized, but we are to appropriate that baptism, to walk it out. I once heard of a man who, before his baptism, drew a stick man representing himself at the bottom of the baptistery before it was filled with water. Ever after, when the old man rose, he could say, "No, I left you in the baptistery. Stay down, stay dead."

When we die, Christ by His Holy Spirit lives through us. That glory of the Father that raised Jesus from the dead (Rom. 6:4), and that is in fact the Holy Spirit (1:4), will manifest Himself in our lives. If we desire more of the Spirit, more of the Father's glory, more of the power of the resurrection, then we must identify more with Christ in His death at Calvary—we must own our own death. This life in the Spirit (Rom. 8) is often squandered by those who have been justified (Rom. 5), because they fail to actualize fully their union with Christ's death through their baptism (Rom. 6—7). Those who break through to the life in the Spirit are those who have broken fully with their old lives. This comes only as we walk to, kneel before, work in, and walk out our Calvary. Be sure, the fellowship with Christ's sufferings will bring the power of the resurrection.

A. J. Gordon, the effective nineteenth-century evangelist and Bible teacher, came into an understanding of the Spirit-filled life following a crisis in his own ministry when he was burned out and signed off work. The Lord came to him and said, "There standeth among you one whom you don't know," and gently led him into an understanding of the life in the Spirit. Gordon began to see that the Holy Spirit had been with him so long and yet he had not known Him. He set to seeking out what union with Christ really meant and entered into a personal, consuming encounter with the Spirit that set the effective trajectory for the rest of his ministry.

Gordon would speak of the gift of the Holy Spirit as the "dynamic of discipleship," but he also said that experiencing this dynamic was costly to our human nature, meaning "even death to self." In one convention address he said,

> *It costs much to obtain the power. It costs self-surrender and humiliation and the yielding up of our most precious things to God. It costs the perseverance of long waiting and the faith of strong trust. But when we are really in that power, we shall find this difference: that whereas before it was hard for us to do the easiest things, now it is easy for us to do the hardest.*[21]

The spiritual writer Gene Edwards also offered this powerfully perceptive insight:

> *If you ever see a great work of God, something joyous, alive and real, something of Christ, something that is Christ, something enduring, then you may be certain of one thing: some lonely*

saint, silent, alone, went to the cross, suffered, died and fell into
the earth. And for what did that someone die, for that lovely
harvest, that work of God, which you now see and declare to be
so beautiful. There must be another day, and another body of
believers. A day when someone else must fall into the earth and
die. And that someone may be you.

THE SPIRIT-LED WAY OF THE WILDERNESS

... for still, I am a willow in the wilderness
Loving the wind that bent me. (Emerson, "Musketaquid")

At His baptism Jesus, the eternal divine Son of God, identifying fully with and for the repentant, receives the assurance of
Sonship from His Father—"This is My Son, in whom I'm well
pleased"—and receives the anointing of the Holy Spirit, who
descends and remains upon Him as a dove. Jesus' earthly ministry will be exercised, not primarily in His own divinity, but in
His Holy Spirit-anointed humanity.[22] "Jesus, full of the Holy
Spirit, returned from the Jordan and was led by the Spirit into
the wilderness ... And Jesus returned to Galilee in the power of the
Spirit and news spread about Him through all the surrounding
synagogues ..." (Luke 4:1, 14).

After Jesus has received the Spirit at baptism, His kingdom
ministry, surprisingly, does not begin immediately. He must go
into the wilderness and there face His adversary. The ensuing
temptations, motivated by the Evil One's hatred for the manifestation of God's Son in the fullness of the Spirit, will center on
whether Jesus will allow Himself to be led by the Spirit or led by

the flesh. Jesus stands firm and resists every temptation, thereby showing that we, too, although we cannot escape temptation, can escape sin.

The Spirit-filled, Satan-thwarting Son of Man then returns "in the power of the Holy Spirit." Why the change in terms from "full of the Holy Spirit" to "in the power of the Holy Spirit"? Is it merely semantic or truly significant? Is Luke purposely making a distinction between the Spirit-filled going into the wilderness and the Spirit-empowered coming out from the wilderness? I believe he is. This Spirit-filling at Jesus' baptism is inextricably linked with a public revelation and private reassurance of His sonship. But the Spirit must take Jesus to a private, desperate, and dangerous place to allow Him to be tested and tempered. Only then does Jesus begin His ministry of preaching and miracles in the power of the Spirit.

I suggest that many Christians, having received the Spirit at conversion, the Spirit of adoption and sonship, have never allowed themselves to be led by that selfsame Spirit into the wilderness. But those who would know the Spirit's power and not just His presence must be tempted, tried, tested, and tempered, so that they might learn to live dependent on God and not on themselves.

The wilderness is a training ground prepared by the Holy Spirit for those who desire to minister in the power of the Spirit. The Spirit may even permit a direct demonic assault upon God's anointed, seeking to knock us out of our destiny, but this is all preparation—as we learn to understand our dependence on God and our obedience to Him, as we recognize and resist the Enemy's assault on our own life before we rout him out of the lives of others. For Jesus, and for us, it is impossible to go on with God without first (and not just once) coming face-to-face with the powers of darkness.

Bunyan's *Pilgrim's Progress* begins with the line, "As I walked through the wilderness of this world ..."[23] The world in his book, for the pilgrim, is a place of transition, affliction, decision, and preparation for the Celestial City. But within this wilderness there are paths to places of crisis and conflict. Following his deliverance at the cross, where his heavy load of guilt and sin was rolled away into the tomb, Christian's progress is by way of the Valley of Humiliation, his desert place. Here he is set upon by the demonic Apollyon (the Destroyer) and fierce conflict ensues. The oppressed Christian eventually overcomes through wielding the two-edged sword of God. But he is a better, stronger, wiser, deeper, and more stable believer for this encounter. Later, Mr. Great-heart, speaking of this valley, says, "This Valley of Humiliation is of itself as fruitful a place as any the crows fly over ..."[24] The Guide says,

> *All states are full of noise and confusion, only the Valley of Humiliation is that empty and solitary place. Here a man shall not be so let and hindered in his contemplation as in other places he is apt to be. This is the valley that nobody walks in but those that love a pilgrim's life. And though Christian had the hard hap to meet here with Apollyon and to enter with him into a brisk encounter, yet I must tell you, that in former times, men have met with angels here, have found pearls here, and have in this place found the words of life.*[25]

Although undesirable, painful, detestable, the wilderness is the making of the men and women of God. Joseph was an anointed and appointed leader, but spent years in his wilderness as a slave and prisoner before he rose to fulfill his destiny (Gen. 37—41), saving his people from famine. Moses was the anointed and appointed deliverer of Israel from birth, but God had to prepare him for forty years in the wilderness near Horeb (Ex. 3:1) before He summoned him to lead Israel out of Egypt. The Israelites were God's chosen people, redeemed out of Egypt by God's mighty hand, but they spent forty years wandering around the wilderness being prepared to enter the Promised Land (Deut. 29:5).

David was God's Spirit-anointed warrior king, but he spent years on the run, hiding in the wilderness of En Gedi before he was eventually crowned king (1 Sam. 24:1). Elijah was God's anointed prophet, but before the great showdown at Carmel and the confrontation with and destruction of pagan worship, he spent three years enduring the pain of his own prophecy (1 Kings 17:1f.), living by a river, fed by the scraps dropped by ravens, eventually resorting to being dependent on a widow for sustenance. John the Baptist was anointed by the Spirit from birth (Luke 1:15), but lived in the desert for several decades until the day of His appearing, preparing for and witnessing to Christ (v. 80). Paul was remarkably converted, filled with the Spirit through Ananias (Acts 9:17f.), and even began an anointed ministry among the Jews of Damascus (vv. 19–22). But God had greater things in store for him, and led Paul into his wilderness in Arabia for three years before he returned in apostolic power of the Spirit (Gal. 1:17–18).[26]

In all these experiences time in the wilderness waste places was never wasted. Wilderness is a place where God's people have less of this world in order to gain more of God. This whole book has been about gaining more of God in our lives: Well, more is less and less is more. The wilderness is where we are emptied of all that clutters our lives, in order to make space and time for more of God. If we are sincere in seeking Him, if we desire a greater empowering of His Spirit for life and ministry, it will not be long before the Spirit leads us into the wilderness.

Throughout the Judeo-Christian tradition, the wilderness has been a significant theme as a place for fashioning and form-ing God's people. In the intertestamental period the Essene and Qumran communities lived in the desert as they tried to purify and refound God's people so as to live rightly in the Promised Land. When the church became institutionalized following Constantine's conversion in the fourth century, many withdrew to the deserts to seek God. The Desert Fathers, founders of the ascetic or monastic life, grew out of this desire for more of God. In many respects the pre-Easter Lenten fasts developed in the church since the post-apostolic era are an attempt to build into our lives a place for God—a wilderness where we may be humbled, honed, hardened, and made more holy.

In the wilderness there are lessons we learn about the nature of sin, ourselves, the Lord, His faithfulness, holiness, righteousness, and powerful Word, and also about our human sinfulness, weak-ness, and utter dependence on Christ to save and sustain. Indeed, there are some lessons that can only be learned in the wilderness. The wilderness does not need to be a specific location set apart: The Spirit may not lead us to a wilderness, but He may lead the wilder-ness to us.

MY UTMOST FOR HIS HIGHEST THROUGH THE DESERT

Oswald Chambers is a name renowned throughout the church. Although he died while still in his forties, his ministry as YMCA chaplain, evangelist, author, preacher, and Bible college principal made a significant impact on a whole generation. But he is best known for a collection of pieces from his talks, published under the title *My Utmost for His Highest*.[27] For nearly a century, his writings have caused Christians throughout the world to seek more of God. He lived what he wrote—he was a man passionate for more of God, passionate to climb the Lord's mountain. But he always taught that this spiritual ascent came through a personal descent, through a laying down of one's life on the altar of God.[28]

While he was a tutor in philosophy at Caloon College, he heard F. B. Meyer speaking on the fullness of the Spirit. Hungry to have what he had heard about, determined to have everything that God had to offer, he returned to his room and asked God to give him simply and definitely this experience of the fullness of the Spirit. Chambers says that from that day on, for four years, nothing but the overruling grace of God and kindness of his friends kept him out of an asylum. Seeking the Spirit, he was taken to the desert.

Although God used him in those years, he had a personal existential crisis, a death experience. God seemed absent, the Bible irrelevant, and he was overwhelmed by the sense of his own sinfulness and depravity as the Spirit shone His searing, purging light into every nook and cranny of his being. Eventually the wilderness experience came to an end—as quickly as it had begun—at an after-church meeting, when he stood and gave public testimony to his sinfulness and desperate need for the Spirit's power, saying that either

Christianity was fraudulent or he had got the wrong end of the stick. Sitting down, he claimed the gift of God on the basis of his promise. There were no angelic visitations, no open heaven, no dramatic revelations, just an assurance that the wilderness was past and he had entered into a new phase of ministry in the power of the Spirit.

The next time he preached, forty people came to Christ. The Spirit's anointing had come to him, and the wilderness was turned to blossom. He now knew a new and deep intimacy with Christ, so as to be able to say later, "If the four previous years had been hell on earth, these five years have been truly heaven on earth. Glory be to God, the last aching abyss of the human heart is filled to overflowing with the love of God. Love is the beginning, love is the middle, and love is the end. After he comes in, all you see is Jesus only, Jesus ever."

The next few years were marked for Oswald Chambers by great authority, writing, traveling and preaching throughout Asia, Africa, Europe, and America. Wherever he went, his message of a surrendered life drew people into greater consecration to God and appropriation of the fullness of the Spirit. He died while working as chaplain to the British troops in Egypt in 1915. On his tomb, in the military cemetery in Cairo, is engraved his name and the promise of Jesus from Luke 11:13, "How much more will your heavenly Father give the Holy Spirit to them that ask Him." And thus his tombstone, a symbol of death, testifies to the promise of life in the Spirit. Chambers knew from personal experience and scriptural evidence that it is only as we die that Christ's power, the "more" of His Spirit, can flow through us.

Let me expand a little now on the features of the wilderness.

1. The wilderness is a place of separation

Through situation and circumstance, God engineers to teach us the principles of wilderness. It may not be a place of physical separation, but it is one of spiritual and existential separation. Jesus had company, but was very lonely: There was no longer the reassuring voice of the Father, just the voice of the tempter.

The wilderness is a place where we travel light. The essence is of being stripped down. We are laid bare of everything that insulates us from or inoculates us against receiving all that God has for us, bringing us to a place of surrender.

Wilderness is going out of your comfort zone—the familiar, comfortable, predictable, and reliable things have been removed. A sense of moral, social, even spiritual dislocation, desolation, and disintegration is not unusual, before God brings His glorious revelation. But the Devil and the wild animals are joined by the angels (Mark 1:13) and we learn that the Comforter is worth more than our discomfort.

2. The wilderness becomes a place of revelation

When David was in the wilderness fleeing from Saul, he turned his natural desire for water into a spiritual desire for God: "O Lord, You are my God, earnestly I seek You, in a dry and weary land where there is no water" (Ps. 63:1). In seeking God, he is given to see something of God: "I have seen You in the sanctuary and beheld Your power and glory." This is remarkable. The sanctuary had not yet been built. Even when it was, as a non-Levite, he could never have been permitted to see it and live. But in the desert, turned to God, David has a vision of the temple sanctuary. He sees God's power and love and glory.

Job declared, "He reveals mysteries from the darkness and brings the deep darkness into light" (12:22). In Hosea, God says, "I will lead her into the wilderness and speak tenderly to her" (2:14). In the wilderness of imprisonment Joseph received divine revelation to interpret dreams; in the wilderness Moses saw the burning bush; in the wilderness Israel saw God and received the law as God alighted on Mount Sinai and spoke; in the wilderness of Horeb, Elijah heard the still small voice of God; in the wilderness of exile the prophets spoke to Israel; in the wilderness the word of the Lord came to John the Baptist (Luke 3:2); in the wilderness of Arabia, Paul received the direct revelation of the gospel that he preached (Gal. 1:11–12, 17).

3. The wilderness is a place of consecration

Here we have a choice: Who will I live for and how will I live? Jesus had to decide whether He would follow the Spirit, the cravings of His assumed human flesh, or the temptations of the Evil One. In the desert we decide whether we will give up on God or go on with Him whatever the cost. In the desert God asks us, "What are you living for?" Jack Ellul said, "The desert is the place where human powers must be renounced." John the Baptist was a voice crying in the wilderness, "Make a highway for the Lord," remove every obstacle to His coming to you. He came preaching repentance. In that desert we take a good look at ourselves, are faced with our sin and challenged to turn around.

4. The wilderness is a place of preparation

Churchill titled one of the volumes of his autobiography as *The Wilderness Years*. In it he spoke of his depression, disillusionment, and sense of failure, his sense of being on the scrap heap. Little did he know that the storm clouds of war were gathering and, far from being on the scrap heap, he was preparing for the greatest challenge and greatest glory of his life, to lead the defense of Great Britain and the defeat of Nazi Germany. Moses came out of the desert ready to lead God's people out of Egypt. David came out of the desert trained to be king. John the Baptist came out of the desert as the greatest prophet of the Lord. Without the wilderness, could they have? Would they have? And we see even our Lord Jesus led into the wilderness filled with the Spirit, but subsequently returning in the power of the Spirit, ushering in God's kingdom.

5. The wilderness is a place of benediction

Although it is a place of correction, pruning, and discipline, God is there in the desert. It is a place of unusual grace. The prophet Jeremiah said, "They found grace in the wilderness" (31:2). God led Israel in the wilderness with a pillar of fire and a pillar of smoke, daily meeting their needs with manna, quail, and water. Their shoes never wore out. The promise of Isaiah is this: "The Spirit is poured upon us from on high and the wilderness becomes a fertile field" (32:15). The desert is God's gift to us—it is the way to more.

In Judges 1:15 we meet the remarkable daughter of Caleb, Achsah. She has been given land by her father, but it is hard, dry, barren land in the Negev—wilderness. She returns to her father and boldly asks, "Give me a blessing. Since you have given me land in the Negev, give me also springs of water." She did not ask to be removed from the desert, she was not bitter or ungrateful for the desert gift, but the desert was not enough. She wanted blessing; she wanted springs. And Caleb gave her the upper and lower springs. When God has given you the desert, don't ask to be taken away from it, ask for a blessing in it—ask Him to give you also springs of water.

The wilderness is a place of favor for the faithful, not torture for the sinful. The sinful may know the absence of a holy God as a direct consequence of their sin and spiritual apathy, but wilderness is a place where God graciously withdraws to test what is in our hearts. Will our hearts press hard after Him? Will they stay loyal to Him? Like the bride in the Song of Solomon (3:1f.), will we seek after Him whom our soul loves although we do not find Him, or will our affection be diverted elsewhere? Will we cry out in loss, in dereliction for the One whose intimacy and tenderness we have known but who has flown? In the wilderness we find out what our hearts desire, and if that is God, we will gain our heart's desire. "What is this coming up from the wilderness, like columns of smoke perfumed with myrrh and frankincense? Behold, it is the traveling couch of Solomon" (Songs 3:6–7). Christ comes to meet us in the desert.

In Hannah Hurnard's classic *Hind's Feet on High Places*, we follow the journey of a young deer—Much-Afraid—who is invited to come to the high places of the mountain but not before she has been led down the valley and through the wilderness. It is a parable of the Christian journey, God's call for us to join Him on His holy mountain, and one chapter is called "Detour through the Desert."

> *"I can't go down there," panted Much-Afraid, sick with shock and fear. "He can never mean that—never! He called me up*

to the High Places, and this is an absolute contradiction of all that He promised." She then lifted up her voice and called desperately, "Shepherd, come to me. Oh, I need You. Come and help me."

In a moment He was there, standing beside her. "Shepherd," she said despairingly, "I can't understand this. The guides You gave me say that we must go down there into that desert, turning right away from the High Places altogether. You don't mean that, do You? You can't contradict Yourself. Tell them we are not to go there, and show us another way. Make a way for us, Shepherd, as You promised."

He looked at her and answered very gently, "That is the path, Much-Afraid, and you are to go down there."

"Oh, no," she cried, "You can't mean it. You said if I would trust You, You would bring me to the High Places, and that path leads away from them. It contradicts all that You promised."

"No," said the Shepherd, "it is not contradiction, only postponement for the best to become possible." [29]

In this book I have been arguing that God, by His Holy Spirit, always has more for us. More intimacy, more revelation, more understanding, more experience, more anointing, more gifting, more service—but that more is not to be found simply by getting into the prayer ministry line. The deep things of God are learned in the fiery furnace of the desert. It is here that He digs deep wells of His Spirit into our life. We receive more of God's Spirit only as we empty out more of our self, and this takes place in the desert.

This is not a popular theology in most Reformed and charismatic circles, but it remains a deeply necessary one. If we are to be all we can be for our Lord, and if we are to gain all that is ours in Christ, then we must follow His lead into the desert and we must embrace it, for from there, the Spirit-led, Spirit-filled believer returns with a vision and a powerful unction of God's Spirit.

CONCLUSION

IN AT THE DEEP END

Throughout this book I have sought to convey through scriptural exposition, personal experience, and study of church history that God always has more to offer than we can ask for or imagine. I believe that a truly biblical theology must lead us to a truly charismatic experience of greater intimacy with Christ and effective ministry for Christ. There is a greater, deeper, closer walk in intimacy, love, and joy with our Lord. There is more anointing, more gifting, more empowering to serve our King more effectively. The more comes by an intensification of the existing presence of the Spirit within us as our desperate hunger leads to a full surrender of our ambitions, affections, possessions—everything to His Lordship. Often the more comes through a crisis brought on by a period of intense personal consecration and dedication to God.

Sometimes the more breaks in like a flood, but it may also be an ever-increasing movement into the depths of God's love and power. The more flows out of the finished work of the cross and, far from undermining it, further mines it of what Christ won for us. This more spills out of our lives and impacts others, pointing them to

Christ. The more is not a one-off experience, but an ever-deepening infusion of God's life in our soul on the basis of the promises and pathways of Scripture.

I cannot sum up all I have been trying to convey better than in a remarkable story from the life of Billy Graham, perhaps the greatest statesman of the evangelical church in the twentieth century and so manifestly used by the Spirit to bring others to a saving faith in Christ. Graham learned the secret of power from on high, of the Spirit-filled life. In 1947 he "surrendered" to God and chose to believe in the authority of Scripture in the face of the critical scholarship that was undermining the resurrection and so on. This was a major turning point and an empowering event in his life. There was another, however, that took place shortly beforehand, in October 1946, when Graham was visiting English church leaders in preparation for his first British evangelistic campaign.[1]

Graham was staying at Hildenborough Hall, and went to listen to Dr. Stephen Olford, a gifted itinerant evangelist and former Second World War chaplain who was speaking there at a youth conference. Olford was preaching from Ephesians 5:18, on the words, "Do not be drunk on wine, but be filled with the Holy Spirit." When Olford finished, Billy Graham approached him and asked him why he did not make an appeal, stating that he would have been the first to come forward in response to the message. Then, says Wirt, Graham said, "You've spoken of something that I don't have. I want the fullness of the Holy Spirit in my life."

Graham told his biographer John Pollock, "I was seeking for more of God with all my heart and I felt that here was a man who could help me. I could sense that Stephen had something in his life

I wanted to capture—he had a dynamic, a thrill, an exhilaration about him."

Graham had to get back to London, but he arranged to spend a couple of days with Olford in Pontypridd, Wales, near the home of Olford's parents. They spent the two days with their Bibles open. On the first day Olford focused on the need to be rooted in the Word through daily personal devotions. Graham prayed, "Lord, I don't want to go on without knowing this anointing You've given my brother." That night Graham preached to a small crowd, but the preaching was mediocre and the results were meager.

On the second day Olford explained further what it meant to be filled with the Holy Spirit, emphasizing that "there is no Pentecost without Calvary" and that "we must be broken" like the apostle Paul, who himself declared, "I have been crucified with Christ." Olford spoke of his own anointing and fullness by the Holy Spirit, who turned his life inside out, declaring that, "Where the Spirit is truly Lord over the life, there is liberty, there is release—the sublime freedom of complete submission of oneself in a continuous state of surrender to the indwelling of God's Holy Spirit."

Olford says that Graham cried out, "Stephen, I see it. That's what I want." His eyes filled with tears. Graham spent the day fasting and seeking God as Olford continued to open up what the Spirit-filled life looked like, involving a "bowing daily and hourly to the sovereignty of Christ and to the authority of the Word." Turning to prayer on his knees, Graham sought the Lord, on the basis of His Word, and found Him as he consecrated his life to Christ. Olford says, "All heaven broke loose in that dreary little room. It was like Jacob laying hold of God and crying, 'Lord, I will not let you go unless you bless me.'"

Some time later Graham exclaimed, "My heart is so flooded with the Holy Spirit," and Olford says they alternately wept and laughed as Graham paced back and forth across the room, saying, "I have it! I am filled! I'm filled. This is the turning point of my life. This will revolutionize my ministry." Olford says that later that night Graham addressed a large Baptist church nearby. "When he arose to preach, he was a man absolutely anointed." They came forward to pray even before the invitation was given—and later, when it was given, nearly the whole church was crammed in the aisles rushing forward.

Olford drove back that night to his parents' home and when he entered the house, his father, a retired missionary, looked at his face and asked, "What on earth has happened?" Olford said that he sat on the kitchen table and told his dad, "Something has happened to Billy Graham. The world is going to hear from this man. He is going to make his mark in history." All Graham's associates recognized this new anointing, new power, new authority, new influence. Here was a man who had sought and fought and caught the more of God! And they were not the only ones to notice: At least a million people have met Christ through Graham's messages, and countless times that number have been renewed and inspired through his ministry. In case you think it was the "experience" that catapulted Graham into ministry, let me make my point clear: It was the lessons he learned and obeyed that brought God's power, as he was daily sustained by the Word, totally surrendered to God.

I hope that this little book will encourage you to seek more of God. I hope that, by following the biblical paths and patterns, you may know fully whom you have believed; know fully the joy unspeakable and full of glory; know fully the love of Christ, which passes all understanding; know fully what it is to be filled to the fullness of God; know fully the Spirit conforming you into Christ's image; and know fully the power from on high to be His effective witnesses.

A Puritan prayer[2]

*Give me a deeper repentance, a horror of sin, a dread of its
    approach;*
*Help me chastely to flee it, and jealously to resolve that my
    heart shall be thine alone.*
*Give me a deeper trust, that I may lose myself to find myself in
    thee,*
The ground of my rest, the spring of my being.
*Give me a deeper knowledge of thyself as Saviour, Master, Lord
    and King.*
*Give me deeper power in private prayer, more sweetness in thy
    Word,*
More steadfastness on its truth.
Give me deeper holiness in speech, thought, action
And let me not seek moral virtue apart from thee.
Plough deep in me, great Lord, heavenly Husbandman,
*That my being may be a tilled field, the roots of grace spreading
    far and wide*
*Until thou alone art seen in me, thy beauty golden like summer
    harvest,*

Thy fruitfulness as autumn plenty.

I have no master but thee, no law but thy will, no delight but
    thyself,

No wealth but that thou givest, no good but that thou blessest,

No peace but that thou bestowest.

I am nothing but that thou makest me, I have nothing but that
    I receive from thee,

I can be nothing but that grace adorns me.

Quarry me deep, dear Lord, and then fill me to overflowing
    with living water.

A prayer by Andrew Murray[3]

My Holy Lord. I bless Thee that the Holy Spirit is in me. But
Oh I beseech Thee, give me yet the full, overflowing measure
Thou hast promised. Let Him be to me the full unceasing
revelation of Thy presence in my heart as glorious and mighty
as on the throne of heaven. Oh my Lord Jesus … fill me with
the Holy Spirit. Amen.

A song by Tim Hughes[4]

There must be more than this:
O Breath of God, come breathe within.
There must be more than this:

Spirit of God, we wait for You.
Fill us anew, we pray;
Fill us anew, we pray.

Consuming fire, fan into flame
A passion for Your name.
Spirit of God, fall in this place.
Lord, have Your way.
Lord, have Your way with us.

Come like a rushing wind.
Clothe us in power from on high.
Now set the captives free;
Leave us abandoned to Your praise.
Lord, let Your glory fall;
Lord, let Your glory fall.

From Morning Prayer, Part of Celtic Daily Prayer— published by Collins

Call: Who is it that you seek?
Response: We seek the Lord our God.
Call: Do you seek him with all your heart?
Response: Amen, Lord have mercy.
Call: Do you seek him with all your soul?
Response: Amen, Lord have mercy.

Call: Do you seek him with all your mind?
Response: Amen, Lord have mercy.
Call: Do you seek him with all your strength?
Response: Amen, Lord have mercy.

From A Diary of Revival by Kevin Adams, CWR Press, Surrey, 2004

This prayer was first recorded in the diary of Evan Roberts on November 10, 1904 – Roberts subsequently sparked and steered the Welsh Revival and this prayer was taught to the congregations and often repeated in the services:

~ Send the Spirit now for Jesus Christ's sake
~ Send the Spirit now powerfully for Jesus Christ's sake
~ Send the Spirit more powerfully for Jesus Christ's sake
~ Send the Spirit still more powerfully for Jesus Christ's sake

Famous hymn of Bianco of Siena (d. 1434)—often used at ordinations

Come down, O love divine, seek Thou this soul of mine,
And visit it with Thine own ardor glowing.
O Comforter, draw near, within my heart appear,
And kindle it, Thy holy flame bestowing.

O let it freely burn, til earthly passions turn
To dust and ashes in its heat consuming;
And let Thy glorious light shine ever on my sight,
And clothe me round, the while my path illuming.

Let holy charity mine outward vesture be,
And lowliness become mine inner clothing;
True lowliness of heart, which takes the humbler part,
And o'er its own shortcomings weeps with loathing.

And so the yearning strong, with which the soul will long,
Shall far outpass the power of human telling;
For none can guess its grace, till he become the place
Wherein the Holy Spirit makes His dwelling.

Prayer by Jim Elliot—martyred by Auca Indians—
recorded in his diary

"God I pray thee, light these idle sticks of my life
and may I burn for thee. Consume my life my God, for it is
thine."

DISCUSSION QUESTIONS

This guide is for individuals and groups who want to go deeper in this book through personal study and/or discussion. If you're studying with a group, the best way to use this guide is to read the chapter, work through the questions yourself, then meet with your group to discuss what you've learned. Some of the questions ask you to examine your life, and if you're meeting with a group of people you don't know well, you might not want to share all the personal details. That's fine. Just be completely honest in your self-examination time, and then share with your group at a level that seems appropriate.

There are generally more questions listed here than a group can dig into deeply in an hour or so, but that gives the leader the freedom to select topics that seem most helpful for the group. In the same way, if you're studying on your own, you can select the questions that point to areas you think God wants you to focus on. The last question for each chapter is a suggestion for prayer, and praying these things for one another in the group can be one of the best things you do for each other.

CHAPTER 1

1. As you begin this book, how would you describe your current thoughts regarding "more" of the Holy Spirit? (Use the options below to prompt your thinking, but don't feel limited by them.)

- I believe I am already experiencing the fullness of the Holy Spirit.
- I feel desperate for something more in my Christian life.
- I am skeptical of teaching that focuses on seeking more of the Holy Spirit.
- I am concerned that those who seek more of the Holy Spirit often do so at the expense of good theology about Christ's finished work on the cross.
- I am concerned about teaching that makes so much of emotional experiences.
- I am pursuing more of the Holy Spirit, but I'm concerned that most Christians I know are not.
- I experience the love of God most of the time and at an increasingly deep level.
- I have experienced a filling of the Holy Spirit in the past, but it's not part of my recent experience.
- I need greater boldness to proclaim Christ.
- I don't think I have as much joy in Christ as I think I should have, given what the New Testament says on the subject.
- I have some besetting sins that I very much want to get rid of, but I'm surprised at the idea that more of the Holy Spirit would make a difference.

- I don't have the kind of "blazing love" for Christ that the author speaks of.
- I'm longing for intimacy with Christ and the fullness of the Holy Spirit.
- I am open to the possibility that I need more of the Holy Spirit, but I'm not sure what that means.
- I _____
- I _____
- I _____
- I _____

2. Simon asks, "If we have what the first Christians had, why do we not do what they did?" How would you respond?

3. a. Rather than a once-only "second blessing," Simon says we need "a constantly repeatable, deepening experience of God's Spirit, who brings a greater revelation of the person and work of Christ, a blazing love for Christ, a greater and more effective empowering witness to Christ, and a transforming conformity to the character of Christ." How much of this do you agree or disagree with, and why?

   b. Consider the above description of what a deeper experience of the Holy Spirit does in a person's life. Does this description sound egocentric? Desirable? Please explain.

4. What do you think Paul means when he prays in Ephesians 3:19 that we may be filled with the fullness of God?

5. What does Simon mean when he says Christ's cross is the door, not the room?

6. a. Would you say your natural temperament and/or upbringing predispose you to be suspicious of or uncomfortable with emotions? If so, how?

   b. Would you say your natural temperament and/or upbringing predispose you to be drawn to dramatic emotions and experiences? If so, how?

   c. Up to now, have you tended to favor deep emotional experience over reason? Reason over deep emotional experience? A union of reason with deep emotional experience? Please explain.

7. How do you respond to Simon's use of the term "biblical deism"—God being absent from the world apart from His Word written, read, or heralded?

8. a. Simon writes, "A nonexperiential religion is suspect, for it fails to deal with the totality of our being." Why does he think it fails to do this?

   b. How do you respond to his argument?

9. Read Psalm 42:1–2 aloud. Then write or speak your own prayer that expands on or responds to this passage. Can you honestly say that your soul thirsts for God? Can you relate to the image

of a desperately thirsty deer? What do you want to say to God right now?

CHAPTER 2

1. This chapter applies the Song of Solomon to our relationship with God. Simon writes, "We need to find the kisses of His mouth more delightful than wine (Song 1:2). We need to be taken to His banquet hall and know that His banner over us is love (2:4). We need to lie on our beds all night looking and longing for His love (3:1)." How do you respond to the idea of seeing your relationship with Christ in terms of this sort of passion?

2. a. Which of the words below describe your current relationship with God? (Choose as many as apply, and feel free to add or substitute your own.)

obedience	love
service	passion
study	intimacy
duty	delight
sound doctrine	closeness

   b. What are the risks of a faith that emphasizes the first column but not the second? The second column but not the first?

3. Simon speaks of three levels of love for Christ: "a mere love that obeys His commands, a love whose heart is constantly fixed on

Jesus, and a love that sets you on fire and all who touch you feel the heat of it." How would you describe the level of love you have for Christ? (Or, do you think speaking in terms of levels is unhelpful?)

4. a. Read John 4:13–14. What do you think Jesus means when He promises that those who drink the water He gives will never thirst again?

   b. Read John 7:37–39. What is Jesus promising to those who come to Him, believe in Him, and drink? Explain what you think His figures of speech mean.

   c. How persistent are you in going to Him and drinking His living water? Why is that? (Or, do you think going to Him, believing in Him, and drinking from Him are meant to be one-time events? Explain.)

5. Simon explains the word *filled* in both Hebrew and Greek, and then shows how various biblical books (especially Luke-Acts) depict people filled with the Spirit. Look up the passages he cites. To what extent do you find his summary of the biblical evidence compelling? From this evidence, what would you say is involved in being filled with the Spirit?

6. a. In Ephesians 5:18, when Paul exhorts his readers to be filled with the Holy Spirit, do you think he is talking to us, too? If so, what does he mean for us to do?

b. Simon says that Ephesians 5:18 "is also the linchpin of a long ethical section running from Ephesians 4:17 to 6:20. Paul is saying that if we are to live a life marked by personal holiness and mutual love, and if we are to fight and stand against the demonic principalities and powers, we must be filled with the Spirit." Do you find this understanding of the text persuasive? Why or why not? What are the implications for us?

7. On what basis might one conclude from the biblical evidence that being filled with the Spirit was meant to be common for first-century Christians but not for us? Or, on what basis might one conclude that we, too, are meant to be filled with the Spirit?

8. Why does Simon believe repentance has to precede filling with the Spirit?

9. a. For you, what are the potential risks and costs of seeking earnestly to be filled with the Spirit?

   b. What are the potential benefits?

10. Simon suggests various things to pray for: "Pray for the longing to long" for Christ. "Ask God to make you all that the Spirit of God can make you, not only a satisfied believer who has drunk for himself, but a useful believer who overflows the neighborhood with blessing..." (Spurgeon). "Offer [yourself] constantly to the Lord to be filled and refilled, so that [you] reach the

fullness of [your] individual capacity." At this point, what will you pray for regarding love for Christ and fullness of His Spirit?

CHAPTER 3

1. Do you need to give more of yourself to the Spirit? If so, what is some of that "more" you need to give?

2. Do you think you should focus on giving more of yourself to the Spirit *instead of* on receiving more of Him and from Him? Please explain.

3. In Colossians 1:9–11, Paul prays:

> *… that you may be filled with the full knowledge of God's will, through all spiritual wisdom and understanding, that you may lead lives worthy of the Lord, fully pleasing Him, as you bear fruit in every good work, and growing in the full knowledge of God with all power, empowered according to the might of His glory with all endurance, longsuffering with joy …*

Pause and pray this for yourself, either word for word or in your own words. What is God inviting you to ask for?

4. Look at Ephesians 1:3–19. Do you agree with Simon that Paul reminds the Ephesians of what they already have (vv. 3–14) and then prays for them to fully avail themselves of it (vv. 15–19)? If

so, what are the implications of Paul's doing that? If not, how do you see the passage differently?

5. Simon argues that we need the Spirit to make real to us what the Bible tells us about God:

- The Bible states that Jesus is Lord, but the Spirit makes that real to me (1 Cor. 12:3).
- The Bible states that God is Father, but the Spirit makes that real to me (Rom. 8:15).
- The Bible states that God is glorious, but the Spirit makes that real to me (2 Cor. 3:15f.).
- The Bible states that God is love, but the Spirit makes that real to me (Eph. 3:16f.).

a. Look up the verses listed above. To what extent do you find Simon's interpretation of the Spirit's role convincing? Why?

b. Which of the truths below are profoundly real to you at an experiential level, and which are not?

Jesus is my Lord.
> God is my Father.
> God is glorious.
> God is love.

c. If you think "real to you at an experiential level" is meaningless or irrelevant, please talk about why.

6. Do you believe God speaks exclusively—or only primarily and normatively—through Scripture? Please explain your thoughts.

7. Simon says "we need the Spirit to take the Word of God and break through those years of lies and sin to help us truly know what [God] has laid up for us in our heavenly chests." Do you think this is part of the Spirit's job? Why or why not?

8. a. Paul declared that the kingdom of God is not a matter of talk but of power (1 Cor. 4:20), and he prays that the Ephesians may know the immeasurable greatness of God's power for us who believe (Eph. 1:19). How do you respond to the idea of Christians praying for the power of the Holy Spirit to work through them?

   b. Are there manifestations of power that some Christians attribute to the Holy Spirit but that you would not want to see in your church or your life? If so, what are they, and why? If you are more comfortable with certain manifestations than others in your discussion group, talk about why.

   c. "This is not power simply for my benefit, but for others." What might this look like? Is this something you want? Why or why not?

9. Pray Ephesians 1:16–19 for yourself and your church:

> *I have not ceased praying for you, remembering you in my prayers, that the God of our Lord Jesus Christ may give you*

three things: the Spirit of wisdom and revelation to fully know Him, having the eyes of your hearts enlightened that you may know what is the hope to which He has called you, the riches of His glorious inheritance in the saints; and the immeasurable greatness of His power for us who believe.

CHAPTER 4

1. When Jesus says, "I am the bread of life; whoever comes will never go hungry" (John 6:35), what do you think He means? How do we come? Is this something we do once or repeatedly?

2. Read Luke 11:5–13. Jesus says the Father is eager to give the Holy Spirit to those who persistently, even impudently, ask Him. What keeps you from persistently asking for the Holy Spirit?

3. Which of the following do you expect from God? Which do you have faith to seek and receive? Which do you not expect or have faith for? Why?

   - I have faith that God will meet me in the solitary desert places if I withdraw with Him in prayer, silence, and meditation.
   - I have faith that God met me when I converted to Christ.
   - I have faith that God will meet me as I study Scripture or sit under sound teaching.

- I have faith that He'll act if I engage in evangelistic work.
- I have faith that God will meet me through baptism, confirmation, the Eucharist, and confession.
- I expect to encounter God abroad in the world when I seek to minister God's lovingkindness and justice to the poor and oppressed.
- I have faith that God will meet me in power, with gifts following, by the Holy Spirit through prayer and the laying on of hands.
- I have faith that I can know God through the pursuit of a virtuous, holy life, lived in radical distinction and separation from the world.

4. "This Holy Spirit, this divine dynamite, is dangerous. He blows where He wills, He goes where He wills, He will take us where He wills, He will break us as He wills, He will make us as He wills, He will use us as He wills" (John 3:8). How willing are you to surrender yourself to the Spirit if this is what He's like? Why?

5. a. Do you have areas of your life that you want to be off-limits from God? If so, you don't have to tell your discussion group what they are, but take a moment to reflect privately and consider what you want to do with those.

   b. Likewise, take some private time to consider whether any unconfessed sin is keeping you from receiving the Spirit of holiness.

6. How do you respond to talk of opposition from demonic forces?

7. Read 1 Corinthians 12:7–11. Do you believe these gifts ought to be commonly used in churches today? On what do you base your belief about this?

8. Do you feel unworthy to have the Holy Spirit work through you or speak to you powerfully? If so, what do you think God says about those feelings of unworthiness?

9. a. Read Philippians 3:7–14. What does Paul want?

   b. How badly does he want it? How can you tell?

   c. To what extent do you share Paul's desire, his passion, and his persistence?

   d. To what extent do you think God wants you to share these things?

10. Are you settling for too little from God? What makes you say that?

11. Pray for yourself Paul's prayer from Ephesians 3:16–21 (NIV):

   > *I pray that out of his glorious riches he may strengthen you with power through his Spirit in your inner being, so that Christ may dwell in your hearts through faith. And I pray that*

you, being rooted and established in love, may have power, together with all the saints, to grasp how wide and long and high and deep is the love of Christ, and to know this love that surpasses knowledge—that you may be filled to the measure of all the fullness of God.

Now to him who is able to do immeasurably more than all we ask or imagine, according to his power that is at work within us, to him be glory in the church and in Christ Jesus throughout all generations, for ever and ever! Amen.

CHAPTER 5

1. "The Spirit of God is His 'specific and particular making of himself present.'" What are some ways in which the Spirit made God present in Old Testament times?

2. The prophets looked forward to a time when the Spirit would be poured out on all flesh (Joel 2:28), when God would place His Spirit within us, transforming hearts of stone into hearts of flesh, and conforming our lives to the righteousness of the law (Ezek. 11:19; 36:26). How was this promise fulfilled on the day of Pentecost (Acts 2)?

3. a. Read Joel 2:28–29, which Peter quotes in Acts 2:17–21. Do you believe this promise was just for the New Testament generation or for us today as well? Why?

b. What are the implications of this for our lives?

4. a. Read John 14:15–26. In this passage, what does Jesus promise that the Spirit will do for His disciples?

  b. In what ways, if any, do you experience the Holy Spirit doing these things?

5. a. Which of the following do you believe the Spirit wants to do for us today?

  - apply the work of Christ at the cross to our lives in justification, regeneration, and sanctification (1 Cor. 6:11)
  - present Christ to us as our Lord (1 Cor. 12:3)
  - glorify Christ to us (John 16:13–14)
  - immerse us into eternal mystical union with Christ (1 Cor. 12:13)
  - anoint us as witnesses to the death, resurrection, ascension, return, and reign of King Jesus (Acts 1:8) with signs following (Rom. 15:19)
  - transform our sinful natures into holy conformity with Christ (2 Cor. 3:17f.; Gal. 5:16–17), preparing us as the bride for Christ's return (Gal. 5:5; Rev. 22:17) as we wait in joy, peace, and hope (Rom. 15:13)

  b. Which of these, if any, would you like Him to do more of in your life?

6. Simon gives several ways of evaluating whether supposed manifestations of the Holy Spirit truly are that. Why are these two important:

- The Spirit will always shine the spotlight on Christ—He
  will always put Christ center stage and manifest Christ
  in His divine Lordship.
- The Holy Spirit did not come for our entertainment or
  excitement, but for our empowerment for evangelism....
  The experience of the Spirit, if authentic, will always
  have an exocentric impulse—propelling us from that
  experience outward to Christ and the world.

7. a. What does Simon mean by "the prophet-hood of all believers
... forthtelling the wonders of God"?

b. Do you find this idea to be true to the biblical evidence? Please
explain.

8. a. What is the value of stillness in Christian life?

b. Why does Simon also urge Christians to be vocal, even loud?

9. a. Kierkegaard said, "Christianity is incendiarism; Christianity is
fire setting; a Christian is a person set on fire." Do you want
to be a person set on fire for love of Christ and witness to the
world? Please explain.

b. Why might a Christian not want that?

10. Simon speaks of physical phenomena accompanying the visitation of the Spirit, such as swooning, crying out, shuddering, falling, lying prostrate and motionless for some hours, shaking, laughing, crying, hands trembling, eyelids fluttering. He also says "the phenomena are somewhat unimportant. We are not to seek such things and we are not to restrict such things. We are to seek the Holy Spirit and look for the fruit of changed and empowered lives."

What do you think about this attitude toward these physical phenomena? Would you find such phenomena acceptable in your church if they went along with changed and empowered lives? Why or why not?

11. a. Simon lists four habits that are essential for the Holy Spirit to move powerfully in an individual or a group of Christians. Why does he believe each is essential?

    • repentance
    • obedience
    • unity
    • prayerfulness

   b. Which of these, if any, present challenges for you? For your church?

   c. On your own, ask yourself: "Is there anything God has asked me to do that I am hesitating about or refusing? Are there any obstacles in my life that are hindering unity with other believers?"

12. What are you willing to pray for? Here are some possibilities:

- Father, send us Your Holy Spirit to apply Christ's work on the cross to our lives, to make us more and more like Him. Transform our sinful natures into holy conformity with Your Son, and prepare us for His return as we wait in joy, peace, and hope.
- Father, send us Your Holy Spirit to help us know and love Christ more deeply as our glorious King.
- Lord Christ, send us Your Holy Spirit to draw us deeper into union with You and the Father.
- Lord, anoint us with Your Holy Spirit as witnesses to Your death, resurrection, ascension, return, and reign. Please give us courage, boldness, and power to declare by our actions and words who You are and what You are doing in the world.
- Father, may Your Holy Spirit reveal to us any areas of sin or disobedience that hinder our love for You or one another.
- Lord Jesus, we want to burn with holy passion for You, passion that moves us out to love and serve the people around us and across the earth. Give us the fullness of whatever You have for us.

CHAPTER 6

1. a. How does Simon define "the baptism in the Holy Spirit"?

b. How does he distinguish it from "the baptism *of* the Holy Spirit" that many Pentecostals speak of?

2. a. Why does Simon insist so strongly that all Christians have been baptized in the Spirit, and that teaching about a second baptism or second blessing is unbiblical?

b. How does he explain the story of the church at Samaria (Acts 8:4–25), in which people come to faith and only later receive the Spirit? To what extent do you find his explanation convincing, and why?

c. How do you respond to the case he makes for "one baptism, many fillings" of the Spirit?

3. Why does he believe his view of "one baptism, many fillings" avoids elitism?

4. If all Christians have been baptized in the Spirit, why do so few of us display the holiness, the boldness, and power for evangelism, and the gifts like prophecy that Simon says the Holy Spirit wants to work in us?

5. Simon says that the fullness God offers us does not come through a one-off experience of God, but through an ongoing entering into all He has given to us in Christ. It involves things such as those listed below. Which of these are already part of your ongoing life? Which need to be more part of your life? Which do you

believe are unnecessary for you? (If there are any that you don't understand, raise your questions with your group.)

- the discipline of prayer
- the discipline of study
- the discipline of worship
- the discipline of giving
- the discipline of consecration
- the discipline of holiness
- the discipline of witness
- ministry and the laying on of hands
- a life lived in obedience
- self-denial and death to the flesh
- revelation by the Spirit and the Word of God

6. What, if anything, do you believe you need to do to lay hold of what is already yours in Christ through the Spirit?

7. If you're prepared to do so, pray for God to release His Holy Spirit within you, whom you have already received by faith in Christ. Your prayer might include these steps recommended by Andrew Murray:

- Step 1—Say "I must be filled"—knowing that God commands it and you need it.
- Step 2—Say "I may be filled"—believing that it is God's promise to all believers.
- Step 3—Say "I should be filled"—willing to surrender all for that pearl of great price.

- Step 4—Say "I shall be filled"—claiming the promised gift of God, purchased by Christ.

CHAPTER 7

1. a. In what ways are the cross and Spirit intertwined in the Scriptures?

   b. Why can't we have the Spirit without the cross?

2. Can you relate to any of these people? If so, how?

   - The tired, dry, weary, worn-down believer whose pilgrimage has substituted drudgery for delight, who must constantly come to the river of life at the place of the skull.
   - The struggling, compromised, backsliding believer who must come back to the river of life at the place of the skull.
   - The desperate believer longing for a greater anointing to serve Christ more effectively who must come to the river of life at the place of the skull.
   - The maturing believer who is longing for a greater, deeper intimacy with the Savior, who must come to the river of life at the place of the skull.

3. a. How does the holiness of the Holy Spirit deal with the temptation to become licentious (unruly, immoral, or unnecessarily eccentric) in the name of being spiritual?

b. At the same time, how does living by the Spirit deal with the temptation to be legalistic in the name of being holy?

c. Are you tempted more by license or by legalism? Please explain.

4. How is it significant to think of baptism as representing death by drowning, rather than just the washing away of sin?

5. a. What does this mean: "God does not want a beautiful alabaster vase set aside to be admired, but a broken one with its contents poured out in worship"?

b. How is this relevant to us?

6. a. What does it mean to consider ourselves dead and to continually crucify our flesh? What does this involve in practice? (Note: Crucifying the flesh does not mean rejecting the body. Jesus had and continues to have a body, and our bodies are created good. The flesh is Paul's term for all that is in us that stands in opposition to God.)

b. Think about the ways in which you are drawn back to the parts of you that should be dead. In what areas do you need to embrace daily crucifixion? Share with your group only if you feel comfortable doing so.

7. a. What is the wilderness experience?

b. How is it valuable?

c. Have you experienced the wilderness? If so, how? If not, how do you respond to the idea that you might need to?

8. Having come to the end of this book, what do you now believe about the idea of seeking more from the Holy Spirit?

9. Throughout this book you've read about people who fasted, prayed, went through wilderness, droughts, and the darkness of God's seeming absence—anything necessary to open themselves to more from the Holy Spirit. What are and aren't you willing to do to seek more from Him? What do you think you need to do, if anything?

10. Choose one or more of the prayers at the end of the concluding chapter as a springboard for your own prayers.

ENDNOTES

INTRODUCTION

1. Kenneth Grahame, *The Wind in the Willows* (London: Egmont Books, 2003), 28–29.
2. There is a long and strong scriptural and church tradition familiar with metaphors for God's presence as a river (Ps. 36:8; 46:4; Is. 41:17f.; 48:18; Ezek. 47:1–10; John 4:13–15; 7:37–39; Rev. 22:1–5) and God's people as fish (Ezek. 47:9–10; Matt. 4:18–19; Luke 5:1–10; John 21:11). Significantly, the Greek word *ichthus* (fish) is an acrostic for "Jesus Christ, God's Son, Savior," and for two thousand years has been a major symbol representing Christians and the church. There are also numerous examples in Scripture where fish have a prophetic as well as a pragmatic function (Ezek. 47:9; Jonah 1—2; Matt. 7:10; 14:17; 17:27f.; Mark 6:38).
3. Frederick William Henry Myers (1843–1901), "Surrender to Christ," *The Oxford Book of Christian Verse* (Oxford: Oxford University Press, 1951), 491.

CHAPTER 1

1. Billy Graham, *The Holy Spirit* (Nashville: Thomas Nelson, 2000).

2. F. Zuendel, *The Awakening* (Rifton, NY: Plough, 1999).

3. Sermon on "Baptism in the Spirit," 25th May 1961.

4. This is a contentious term and concept that we will be exploring throughout the book, notably in chapter 6. Let me simply say here that I believe the term is the wrong one: Baptism in the Spirit, mentioned in all the Gospels and twice in Acts, is shown in 1 Corinthians 12:13 to be conversion to Christ and incorporation into His church. I personally prefer to call the ongoing experience of the Spirit "the fullness of the Spirit" (see Eph. 3:19; 5:18). Whatever the term, the ongoing experience is the right and necessary one that we may know and must seek.

5. See a very helpful discussion of this whole issue and a summary of Lloyd-Jones' thought in the significant book by Stuart Piggin, *Firestorm of the Lord* (Carlisle, UK: Paternoster Press, 2000), 98. Lloyd-Jones' own writings on this are most notably found in *Joy Unspeakable* (Eastbourne, UK: Kingsway, 1984), 91f.

6. Sermon titled "Tongues of Fire and the Fullness of God," 14th October 1990.

7. Translation by Raniero Cantalamessa in his outstanding book, *Come Creator Spirit* (Collegeville, MN: The Liturgical Press, 2003), 5. The whole book is a remarkable commentary on this ancient hymn. For an alternative translation see Jürgen Moltmann, *The Spirit of Life* (London: SCM, 1992), 311.

8. See John Capon, *John and Charles Wesley* (London: Hodder and Stoughton, 1988), 71f., 99f.

9. John Pollock, *Billy Graham* (London: Hodder and Stoughton, 1966), 46.

10. Emil Brunner, *The Divine Imperative* (Cambridge, UK: Lutterworth Press, 1937), 565.

11. Both these are useful evangelical gospel tracts.

12. For a systematic treatment of this theme, see Brian Gaybba, *The Spirit of Love* (London: Geoffrey Chapman, 1987), especially 59–66, 78–87, 128–137, 141f.

13. Eduard Schweizer, *Spirit of God* (London: A & C Black, 1960), 24, from the series Bible Key Words from Gerhard Kittel's *Theologisches Wörterbuch zum Neuen Testament.*

14. This is not too dissimilar from the liberals in their demythologizing principle, a term coined by Bultmann in the early part of the twentieth century, describing the method of removing all forms of the miraculous from Christ's ministry, due to an a priori empirical rationalism.

15. Bernard of Clairvaux, *Talks on the Song of Songs,* ed. Bernard Bangley (Orleans, MA: Paraclete Press, 2002), 2. See commentary by Kilian McDonnell, *The Other Hand of God* (Collegeville, MN: Liturgical Press, 2003), 181f.

16. McDonnell, *Other Hand,* 176f.

17. Jonathan Edwards, "Treatise Concerning the Religious Affections," in *Select Works of Jonathan Edwards* (Edinburgh: Banner of Truth, 1961).

18. Gaybba, *The Spirit of Love,* 257.

19. John Piper, sermon on Ephesians 5:18, "Be Filled with the Holy Spirit," 8th March 1981. This sermon, with others of Piper's, is found on the Web site: www.soundofgrace.com/piper.

20. John McIntyre, *The Shape of Pneumatology* (Edinburgh: T. & T. Clark, 1997), 2, 16f.

21. Karl Barth, *The Word of God and the Word of Man* (Gloucester, MA: Peter Smith Publisher, Inc., 1958), 25.

CHAPTER 2

1. John Donne, "Holy Sonnet XV," *The Complete Works* (New York: Everyman Library, 1985), 444.

2. See earlier discussion with reading suggestions, chapter 1.

3. This interpretation has a long and strong history and can be further supported by numerous allusions in the Old Testament to Israel as the bride of God (Isa. 61; Ezek. 16; Hos. 1—14) and in the New Testament to the church as the bride of Christ (Eph. 5; Rev. 21:9).

4. In V. R. Edman, *They Found the Secret* (Grand Rapids, MI: Zondervan, 1984), 69.

5. Stanley Burgess, ed., *The Holy Spirit, Medieval, Roman Catholic and Reformation Traditions* (Peabody, MA: Hendrickson Publishers, 1997), 57. Since Origen, a huge commentarial tradition has surrounded this text. Gregory the Great popularized Origen's allegorical reading of it, and the medieval period saw an abundance of commentary on it, often regarding it as the most elevated text in the canon; see D. Turner, *Eros and Allegory—Medieval Exegesis of the Song of Songs* (Kalamazoo, MI: Cistercian Publication: 1995). Even if not to be taken allegorically, it is a wonderful illustration of the revelation of love between Christ and His bride the church; see G. Lloyd Carr, *The Song of Solomon,* Tyndale OT Commentaries (Downer's Grove, IL: IVP, 1984), 21f.

6. Bernardi Opera, *Sermons Super Cantica Canticorum* 1–35, ed. Leclerg OSB, C. H. Talbot, A. M. Rochais (Rome, 1957), 1.118, 20.v.9.154f.

7. Kilian McDonnell, *The Other Hand of God* (Collegeville, MN: Liturgical Press, 2003), 178.

8. Richard Rolle, *The English Writings,* ed. R. S. Allen (Mahwah, NJ: Paulist Press, 1988), 169.

9. Ibid., 171.

10. From Herman Hesse, *Narcissus and Goldmund* (New York: Noonday Press, 1988).

11. *Works of Richard Sibbes,* 6 vols. (Edinburgh: Banner of Truth, 1973), Vol. 3 453–456.

12. *Letters of Samuel Rutherford* (Sand Springs, OK: Puritan Paperbacks, 1973), 51.

13. See the definitive biography by George Marsden, *Jonathan Edwards: a Life* (New Haven, CT: Yale University Press, 2003), 248.

14. Ibid., 245.

15. This deliverance from depression was God's grace, but sometimes the reverse is the case—see chapter 7.

16. Robert Backhouse, ed., *The Classics on Revival* (London: Hodder and Stoughton, 1996), 249; quote and background details in W. H. Harding, *Finney's Life and Lectures* (Grand Rapids, MI: Zondervan, 1956), 2f.

17. Leon Morris, *Gospel of John*, NICNT (Grand Rapids: Eerdmans, 1984), 420, notes.

18. In John 7:38, Jesus actually says, "Out of you will flow streams of living water." Not only does this river of living water establish the guarantee of eternal life and the means to satisfy a thirsty life, but the "outward" direction of the flow implies a transforming, blessing, and satisfying through us to others. This is not merely for our own well-being—we are to be a well from which others may access that deep river of God.

19. Ps. 107:4–6; Isa. 35:6f.; 41:18f.; 43:20; Ezek. 47:3–12.

20. *The Treasury of the New Testament* (London: Marshall, Morgan and Scott, 1933), as quoted in Blackhouse *Classics on Revival.*

21. Recorded in Brian Edwards, *Revival* (Evangelical Press, 1997), p. 54.

22. There are few references in the Old Testament to being filled with the Spirit, though perhaps a parallel phrase that occurs more frequently is that of "the Spirit coming upon/being upon" (e.g., Num. 24:2; 27:18; Judg. 3:10; 1 Sam. 10:6, 10; 16:13; Isa. 11:2; 61). Those who experienced such a thing included Moses, seventy elders, Balaam, Joshua, Othniel, Jephthah, Saul, Samson, David, Azariah, Jehaziel, Zechariah, as well as Joseph and Daniel. The manifestations of the Spirit under the new covenant are often similar to those in the old, but one key difference is that of universality—no longer the few elite leaders, but the whole elect community.

23. F. F. Bruce, *The Book of Acts,* NICNT (Grand Rapids, MI: Eerdmans, 1989), 92. Bruce notes that the aorist passive participle here indicates a special (subsequent filling) moment of inspiration.

24. Elsewhere we see Jesus sitting at God's right hand. Why here is He standing? Perhaps Jesus got up to greet Stephen, who would soon join Him in glory.

25. See Andrew Lincoln, *Ephesians,* Word Biblical Commentaries (Nashville: Word, 1990), 344, for a useful discussion on the Jewish background to the concept of being drunk religiously.

26. Samuel Chadwick, *The Way to Pentecost* (London: Hodder and Stoughton, 1939), 15.

27. Ernest Best, *ICC on Ephesians* (Edinburgh: T. & T. Clark, 1998), 328.

28. Fuller details of Murray's four steps can be found in Robert Backhouse's *Classics on Revival* (London: Hodder and Stoughton, 1996), 334f.

29. Original sermon material by A. W. Tozer, collected in *How to be Filled with the Holy Spirit* (Camp Hill, PA: Christian Publications, 1992).

CHAPTER 3

1. Martyn Lloyd-Jones, *Revival* (Wheaton, IL: Crossway Books, 1987), 261.
2. V. R. Edman, *They Found the Secret* (Grand Rapids, MI: Zondervan, 1984), 76.
3. In Leon Suenens, *A New Pentecost* (London: Darton, Longman and Todd, 1976), 9.
4. Abridged quote—full quote in Backhouse, *Classics on Revival,* 94f.
5. *Whitefield's Journals,* 9th October 1739 (Edinburgh: Banner of Truth, 1960).
6. For further reading see ed. Stanley Burgess, *The Holy Spirit* (Edinburgh: Hendrickson, 1997), 149f.; Alistair Heron, *The Holy Spirit* (London: Marshall, Morgan and Scott, 1993), 105.
7. *Kerygma* is the noun form meaning "the original apostolic content of the gospel that was preached."
8. Backhouse, *Classics on Revival,* 97.
9. John Stott, *Your Confirmation* (London: Hodder and Stoughton, 1960), 75.
10. James S. Stewart, *Heralds of God* (London: Hodder and Stoughton, 1952), 95.
11. A. Chester Mann, *Moody: Winner of Souls* (London: Marshall, Morgan and Scott, 1936), 52–61.
12. Winkie Pratney, *Revival* (Lafayette, LA: Huntington House Publishers, 1994), 114f.
13. *The Promise of the Spirit* (London: The Epworth Press, 1960),104.

CHAPTER 4

1. C. S. Lewis, *The Last Battle* (New York: HarperCollins, 1998), 181f.

2. Currently he is a director of the Church Missionary Society and author of *The Y Course* and *Beyond Belief*, published by Word.

3. Richard Foster has produced a remarkable work that analyzes the various "streams" of spirituality—Holiness, Sacramental, Charismatic, Contemplative, and Social Justice—and that presents a brief overview of their heart and offers analysis of their respective strengths and weaknesses. See *Streams of Living Water* (New York: HarperCollins, 1998).

4. Ibid., xv.

5. Samuel Chadwick, *The Way to Pentecost* (London: Hodder and Stoughton, 1939), 122.

6. Told by Joel Carpenter, *Revive Us Again* (Oxford: Oxford University Press, 1997), 222; and Sherwood Eliot Wirt, *Billy* (Wheaton, IL: Crossway Books, 1997), who differs on some details but whose main content is the same.

7. His remarkable story is told in David Du Plessis and Bob Slosser, *A Man Called Mr. Pentecost* (Alachua, FL: Bridge Logos Publishers, 1980).

8. See chapter 2.

9. Cardinal Suenens, *Renewal and the Powers of Darkness* (London: Darton, Longman and Todd, 1983), 57–58.

10. St. Augustine, *Expositions of the Psalms,* Ps. 144:1. All available at www.ccel.org/fathers2/NPNF1-081.

11. Source unknown.

12. See Num. 34; Gen. 12:5; 23:2; Ex. 16:35; Deut. 32:49; Josh. 14:1.

13. At a popular and practical level, the most widely used books would be Denis and Rita Bennet, *The Holy Spirit and You* (Alachua, FL: Logos Publishers, 1982); David Pytches, *Come Holy Spirit* (London: Hodder and Stoughton, 1985); Mark Stibbe, *Know*

Your Spiritual Gifts (Grand Rapids, MI: Zondervan, 2000). The standard serious textual approach is by Max Turner, *The Holy Spirit and Spiritual Gifts in the NT Church and Today* (Carlisle, UK: Paternoster, 1998). A fresh dogmatic analysis is found in Donald Bloesch, *The Holy Spirit—Works and Gifts* (Downer's Grove, IL: IVP, 2000).

14. I heard him tell this story to a group of ministers at my home church in Nailsea in 1990. It made a deep impression upon me then and still does today.

15. Cornwall is not negating those other things that God gave and did in his church. Make no mistake, he is not saying that the "gospel" is a mere trinket and we must advance beyond it to a higher plane. By no means—that would be Gnostic and demonic. All I deduce from this story is that God was encouraging his church to receive even more gifting, revelation, encounter, and power from Him, which He was longing to give, but they would not receive it—they settled for too little.

16. The name Jacob means "he grasps by the heel" or "he cheats," and he certainly lived up to his name.

17. A whole industry has sprung up around Jabez, with encouragement to pray the prayer of Jabez and purchase lots of items marketed to help us do this. Much of this worries me as being consumerist in its presentation and even a little cultish and magical in its application. We are not simply to copy the specific intercession of Jabez, repeating his words as if those words per se have inherent power like some occult mantra. Rather we are to have the same motivation as Jabez—to refuse the status quo of our situation; and the same direction as Jabez—looking in prayer to God; and the same passion—to know an extending of God's blessing on our life.

18. A. W. Tozer, *Of God and Men* (Camp Hill, PA: Christian Publications), 14.

19. John Durham, *Exodus,* Word Biblical Commentary (Nashville: Word Publishers, 1987), 440.

20. Vincent Donovan, a Catholic missionary, had to challenge this view in his work amongst the Masai, recounted in *Christianity Rediscovered* (London: SCM Press, 2001). When Donovan asked a Masai warrior where God was, the warrior took him to the highest hill and pointed to the farthest point in the sky.

21. "Whenever" implies repetition, not a single occurrence.

22. Gerald Hawthorne, *Word Biblical Commentary on Philippians* (Nashville: Word, 1991), 138.

23. Arnold Dallimore, *George Whitefield* (Edinburgh: Banner of Truth Trust, 1969), vol. 1, 75f.

24. Some think of this breakthrough as his conversion, and indeed Whitefield understands it in those terms. But I cannot hold with that. He believed, loved, and served God in Christ long before. But there was a privation of intimacy, assurance, and power. That is what came into his life that day. He felt it was a conversion because it was so life-transforming, and the contrast with what went before so marked. But it appears to me, from the language expressed, that it was simply what some term the "baptism in the Spirit," the "filling of the Spirit." Whether it was a conversion or a subsequent blessing is of little matter, however. What matters is the quality, reality, intensity, and fruit of the event, which is so absent in many who profess Christ but do not yet experience this biblical blessing. (See Dallimore, 77.)

25. Arnold Dallimore, *George Whitefield* (Edinburgh: Banner of Truth Trust, 1969), vol. 1, 18.

CHAPTER 5

1. John Donne, "The Litanie," lines 19, 24, in *The Complete English Works* (New York: Everyman Library, 1985), 457.

2. Alistair Heron, *The Holy Spirit* (London: Marshall, Morgan and Scott, 1993), 9.

3. Known personally by the mere few priests, prophets, judges, and kings.

4. The Greek preposition *en* is usually understood as a locative "in," although it can also be an element "with."

5. While Mark 1:8 and John 1:33 simply refer to Jesus baptizing in the Holy Spirit, both Matthew (3:11) and Luke (3:16) add the additional predicate "fire" to the baptism from Jesus. Baptism in the Spirit and fire is a *hendiadys* and does not imply two separate or distinct experiences through or activities of Christ. Fire is a classic theophanic form and may simply imply baptism in the Spirit who is fire. Fire is also a symbol of judgment and, alongside the adjective "holy" Spirit, may simply imply a purging and purifying work by the Holy Spirit who makes us holy. Linked to 3:17b, "the burning up of the chaff," some have suggested that Jesus will come either with the blessing of the Spirit or with the burning of judgment, although John makes it clear that baptism is in/with the Holy Spirit and fire, not the Holy Spirit or fire.

6. See Joachim Jeremias's classic study on numbers and origins of pilgrims, *Jerusalem in the Time of Jesus* (London: SCM, 1974), 58–84, where he gives estimates of pilgrims ranging from 125,000 to 3 million, and travelling from as far afield as Ethiopia and Germany—wherever Diaspora Jews had settled.

7. The word *pentecost* comes from the Greek *pentekostos*, which means "fifty."

8. See Lev. 23:15f.; Deut. 16:9f. Also see F. F. Bruce, *The Book of Acts*, NICNT (Grand Rapids, MI: Eerdmans, 1989), 49f.

9. Wind/breath (*pneuma*) and fire are familiar theophanic forms of God's manifestation (2 Sam. 22:16; Job 37:10; Ezek. 13:13).

10. From S. Kierkegaard, *The Instant*, and *Journals and Papers*, IV, pp. 251f., 549f., in *Provocations, Spiritual Writings of Kierkegaard* (Rifton, NY: Plough, 1999), xix; 334f.

11. James Stuart Stewart, *Heralds of God* (London: Hodder and Stoughton, 1946), 220.

12. See John Stott, *The Message of Acts,* BST (Downer's Grove, IL: IVP, 1991), 62, for an interesting discussion along these themes— although Stott is not convinced himself whether such symbolism is intended to be drawn by Luke.

13. Peter adds the word "my" in his sermon, but the original in Joel 2:29 simply states male and female slaves and refers to the slaves in service to the Israelites. See Hans Conzlemann, *The Acts of the Apostles* (Minneapolis: Fortress Press, 1987), 20.

14. Steven J. Land, *Pentecostal Spirituality* (London: Sheffield Academic Press, 2003), 17.

15. "The Apostolic Faith," December 1907, p. 1, cited in Richard Foster, *Streams of Living Water* (New York: HarperCollins, 1998), 119.

16. Watchman Nee, *The Normal Christian Life* (Eastbourne, UK: Kingsway, 1981), 84f.

17. *The Journal of John Wesley,* 25 May 1738. Full text available online at www.ccel.org/w/wesley/journal.

18. Roger Stronstad, *The Prophethood of all Believers* (London: Sheffield Academic Press, 1999).

19. Samuel Chadwick, *The Way to Pentecost* (London: Hodder and Stoughton, 1939), 10.

20. W. H. Harding, *Finney's Life and Lectures* (Grand Rapids, MI: Oliphants, 1956), 4.

21. K. P. Yohanan, *Revolution in World Missions* (GFA Publications, 2001), 38–48.

22. Karl Barth, *Church Dogmatics* IV.2 (Edinburgh: T. & T. Clark, 1989), 130.

23. Brother Yun, *The Heavenly Man* (London: Monarch Books, 2002), 33f.

24. Ibid., 40.

25. Bruce, *The Book of Acts,* 36.

26. One thinks of John Wesley, who went as a missionary to the Americas but failed miserably because he did not know the power of God and trusted in his own message and his own might. What a difference that day made in Aldersgate, equipping a brilliant but previously powerless man to ride 200,000 miles over the next fifty years preaching Christ.

27. Promise comes from the Latin *pro-mittere,* meaning "to send before"; mission from *mittere,* "to send."

28. Kilian McDonnell, ed., *Towards a New Pentecost for a New Evangelisation,* Malines Document 1 (Collegeville, MN: Liturgical Press, 1993), 1, 64.

29. Hendrikus Berkhof, *Christian Faith* (Grand Rapids, MI: Eerdmans, 1979), 412.

30. Andrew Murray, *The Spirit of Christ* (Hertfordshire, UK: Nisbet & Co., 1888), 160. Reprinted by Bethany House, 1984.

31. Kenneth Latourette, *A History of Christianity* (London: Eyre & Spottiswoode, 1955), 897, 1018, 1025, 1047.

32. Henry Chadwick, *The Church in Ancient Society* (Oxford: Clarendon Press, 2001), 190.

33. Peter Brierley, *The Tide is Running Out* (Christian Research Publications, 1998).

34. Chadwick, *The Way to Pentecost,* 29.

35. Praying Hyde, *The Sunday School Times Company,* 1923, p. 24.

36. Jesus was the preeminently anointed of the Spirit, and His title "Christ" simply means anointed. See Isa. 61:1.

37. The repetition in Jesus' prayer of *hina* (Greek) denotes purpose, aim, or goal—in that order. BAGD p. 376 shows how each successive clause is the consequence of the former, i.e., "I pray for unity, in order that you may indwell God, in order that the world may believe."

38. Leon Morris, *The Gospel According to John,* NICNT (Grand Rapids, MI: Eerdmans, 1984), 734.

39. See also 1 Sam. 12:18; Isa. 29:23; Matt. 9:8; Luke 5:26; 7:16.

40. Told by John Chapman, source unknown.

41. V. R. Edman, *They Found the Secret,* 52.

42. Karl Barth, *Evangelical Theology* (Edinburgh: T. & T. Clark, 1979), 58.

43. Martyn Lloyd-Jones, *Joy Unspeakable* (Eastbourne, UK: Kingsway, 1994), 370.

44. R. B. Jones, *Rent Heavens* (Stanley Martin & Co., 1930), 35.

CHAPTER 6

1. See Rene Laurentin, *Catholic Pentecostalism* (London: Darton, Longman and Todd, 1977), 33, for a discussion of the differences in the Greek text.

2. Here in Acts 11:15, Peter does use the definite article—but the meaning remains identical to that of the other citations.

3. Lloyd-Jones, *Joy Unspeakable,* 332.

4. In John 14:6, Jesus says He is the Truth, then He says He will send
   the Spirit of Truth (John 14:16–17). In John 14:16, Jesus promises
   to send the Holy Spirit, another Comforter, implying that He was
   also the comforter. In John 14:16 the Spirit will be with them
   forever, but in Matthew 28:20 Jesus promises to be with them
   forever. In Romans 8:9–10 we read of both the Spirit of God and
   the Spirit of Christ dwelling with the believer. In Romans 8:27 it is
   the Spirit interceding for the saints, whereas in Romans 8:34, Jesus is
   interceding for us. All these, and many more besides, emphasize the
   mutuality and interchangeability of divine actions and predicates.

5. Gordon Fee, *Commentary on 1 Corinthians*, NICNT (Grand
   Rapids, MI: Eerdmans, 1989), 606.

6. David Pawson, *Jesus Baptises in One Holy Spirit* (London: Hodder
   and Stoughton, 1997).

7. Ibid., 103.

8. Thanks to my father for explaining this threefold view of baptism.

9. Fee, *Commentary on 1 Corinthians*, 603.

10. Pawson, *Jesus Baptises in One Holy Spirit*, 101.

11. Donald Pickerill, "Running Commentary on 1 Corinthians," *The
    Spirit Filled Life Bible* (Nashville: Thomas Nelson, 1991), 737.

12. Pawson, *Jesus Baptises in One Holy Spirit*, 188f.

13. They were not very good disciples of John, as they had not
    grasped the provisional nature of his baptism, which John saw as
    preparatory for the coming of Jesus and baptism in the Spirit. They
    seem to be ignorant of this.

14. John Stott's commentary *The Message of Acts* has an extended
    discussion on this and seems to me convincing; see pp. 151–159.

15. I am not including Acts 12:24, which is a general description about
    the word of God spreading and multiplying, even though this

implies conversions, as it is a rather vague text and not clear on where it happened, though probably Jerusalem. Acts 2:41, three thousand added at Pentecost; 2:47, numbers daily added to the church; 6:7, many priests; 8:4f., Samaritans; 8:26, Ethiopian eunuch; 9:1., Saul; 9:32f., residents of Lydda and Sharon; 10:44f., Cornelius's household; 11:19, Antioch; 13:12, the proconsul in Cyprus; 13:38, Gentiles in Antioch; 14:1f., Iconium; 14:8f., Lystra; 16:1f., Derbe; 16:11f., Lydia's household; 16:25f., Philippian jailor's household; 17:1f., Thessalonica; 17:10f., Berea; 17:16f., Athens; 18:8, Corinth; 19:1f., twelve in Ephesus; 19:17, many in Ephesus.

16. A term offered by Peter Hocken, *The Glory and the Shame* (Eagle Press, 1994), 61.

17. Recalled in Walter Hollenweger, *The Pentecostals* (London: SCM, 1972), 333.

18. Rene Laurentin, *Catholic Pentecostalism*, 47.

19. Raniero Cantalamessa, *Come Creator Spirit* (Collegeville, MN: Liturgical Press, 1993), 54–55.

20. Stott, *The Message of Acts*, 154.

21. Jim Packer, *Keep in Step with the Spirit* (Downer's Grove, IL: IVP, 1984), 76, 78.

22. Discussed and quoted in Walter Hollenweger, *The Pentecostals* (Peabody, MA: Hendrickson, 1988), 335.

23. James Dunn, *Baptism* (London: SCM, 1970), 54.

24. See further commentary in chapter 2 on this imperative, passive, iterative statement of Paul's.

25. Harold W. Hoehner, *Ephesians—An Exegetical Commentary* (Ada, MI: Baker, 2003), 705.

26. W. H. Griffiths-Thomas, *The Holy Spirit of God* (Church Book Room Press, 1913), repr. 1972, 277.

27. P. T. O'Brien, *The Letter to the Ephesians: Pillar Commentary Series* (Downer's Grove, IL: Apollos Press, 1999), 265.

28. Andrew Lincoln, *Ephesians Word Biblical Commentary* (Nashville: Word Books, 1990), 214f.

29. Jack Hayford, "Notes on Ephesians 2:10," *The Spirit Filled Life Bible,* 1791.

CHAPTER 7

1. For the medical significance of the blood and water, see Josh McDowell, *Evidence that Demands a Verdict* (Here's Life Publishers, 1986), 198f.

2. I am talking of the two streams in an allegorical, though deeply theological, sense, but I recognize that the river of the Spirit (water) that brings deep satisfaction is at the same time that which also brings or applies to the believer the river of the blood for our cleansing and salvation. We must avoid making too clear a bifurcation between the two.

3. G. W. H. Lampe, *The Seal of the Spirit* (London: SPCK, 1967), 308.

4. Steven J. Land, *Pentecostal Spirituality* (London: Sheffield Academic Press, 2003), 92.

5. Thomas Smail, *Reflected Glory* (London: Hodder and Stoughton, 1975), 105.

6. Larry Kreitzer, *The Gospel According to John* (Regent Studies, 1994), 65.

7. Jesus' command to them to "wait" (Greek *perimenein*) for the Spirit's coming (Acts 1:4) stems from the same verb (*meno*) as that describing their "waiting" (*katamenontes*) in the upper room (Acts 1:13). Luke tells us in 1:14 that here in this upper room they

were "all together with one mind" (*pantes homothumadon*), which is picked up again (2:1) when they were "all together" (*pantes homou*). Thus a strong semantic link can be established between the upper room where they celebrated the Passover, where they were instructed to wait for the Spirit, which they did all together, and where they subsequently were gathered all together when the Spirit came and filled them.

8. Lyrics from Matt Redman's "You Led Me to the Cross." Copyright 1999 Thankyou Music.

9. Teresa of Avila, quoted in Lucy Lethbridge and Selina O'Grady, eds., *A Deep but Dazzling Darkness* (London: Darton, Longman and Todd, 2002), 65.

10. William Willimon, "Repent," in *Bread and Wine* (Rifton, NY: Plough, 2003), 9.

11. Dietrich Bonhoeffer, *The Cost of Discipleship* (London: SCM, 1959). Note especially the classic chapter on the cross-shaped nature of discipleship, pp. 76–83, from which this quote comes.

12. Søren Kierkegaard, *The Journals of Kierkegaard,* ed. Alexander Dru, (Harper and Brothers, 1959), 245. This theme is discussed with great insight in Richard Foster's chapter "The Prayer of Relinquishment" in his *Prayer* (London: Hodder and Stoughton, 1993), 48–58.

13. Smail, *Reflected Glory,* 105.

14. Roy Hession, *The Calvary Road* (Fort Washington, PA: Christian Literature Crusade, 1982).

15. For theological reflection see Stuart Piggin, *Firestorm of the Lord* (Carlisle, UK: Paternoster, 2000), 75f.

16. Hession, *The Calvary Road,* 11.

17. Ibid., 7.

18. Mark Stibbe, *Revival* (London: Monarch, 1998), 170–174, 210–217.

19. G. Hawthorne, *Word Biblical Commentary* (Nashville: Word, 1991), 148.

20. I am indebted to the wonderful book by Dallas Willard, *Renovation of the Heart* (Colorado Springs, CO: NavPress, 2002), for this illustration as well as for deepening my own understanding of the significance of this spiritual necessity.

21. Edman, *They Found the Secret,* 71–77.

22. Acts 10:38. This often raises theological eyebrows, but according to the canon of Scripture, and with the possible exception of His instructing the teachers at the temple on His religious coming of age, though eternally divine, Jesus' ministry does not start until He takes up His office as the Christ, the Anointed One. Now, only with the Spirit of the Lord anointing Him post-baptism, is He sent to preach the good news to the poor, proclaiming release to the captives, recovery of sight to the blind, and so on (Luke 4:18).

23. John Bunyan, *The Pilgrim's Progress* (New York: Collins, 1971), 25.

24. Ibid., 245.

25. Ibid., 247.

26. Some scholars believe that Paul probably went to Arabia on mission, rather than to commune with God, but there is no other evidence of this, no church planted, no letters written, no further apostolic pastoral visits, and if he did go there on mission, it was the only place Paul visited but never made an impact worthy of note in the New Testament! See F. F. Bruce, *Galatians* (Carlisle, UK: Paternoster Press, 1982), 96. Bruce errs on the side of mission rather than communion.

27. Numerous editions of this are available through the Oswald Chambers Publications Association. It is claimed that this is the most widely published Christian book ever. The definitive account of his life is by David McCasland, *Oswald Chambers—Abandoned to God* (Uhrichsville, OH: Discovery House Press, 1998). I am drawing on V. R. Edman's stirring account in *They Found the Secret,* 44–48.

28. See his writings in *My Utmost for His Highest,* e.g., 11th Jan.; 5th and 6th Feb.; 2nd Sept.; 3rd Nov.

29. Hannah Hurnard, *Hind's Feet on High Places* (Carol Stream, IL: Tyndale House, 1976), 67f.

CONCLUSION

1. This story is taken from Sherwood Eliot Wirt, *Billy* (Wheaton, IL: Crossway Books, 1997), 28–30. Wirt was founding editor of Graham's *Decision* magazine, a lifetime close friend and colleague who expands on John Pollock's account in the authorized biography *Billy Graham* (Hodder and Stoughton, 1966), 62–63, with the benefit of personal letters from Olford and no doubt inside information from Graham.

2. Arthur Bennett, "The Deeps," *The Valley of Vision: Puritan Prayers and Devotion* (Edinburgh: Banner of Truth, 1988), 135.

3. Andrew Murray, *The Spirit of Christ* (Hertfordshire, UK: Nisbet & Co., 1888), 32.

4. Tim Hughes, "Consuming Fire," Copyright 2002, Thankyou Music, EMI Christian Music Publishing.

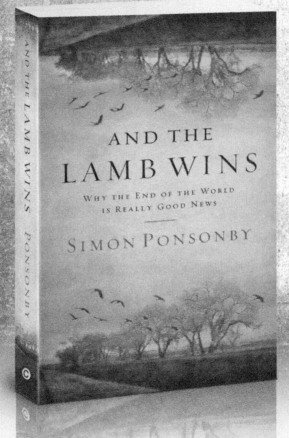